A Village
in the
Shadows

The remarkable story
of St Davids, Ontario

DOROTHY WALKER

 FriesenPress

Suite 300 - 990 Fort St
Victoria, BC, V8V 3K2
Canada

www.friesenpress.com

Published by Dorothy Walker

ISBN
978-1-5255-2251-2 (Hardcover)
978-1-5255-2252-9 (Paperback)
978-1-5255-2253-6 (eBook)

1. HISTORY, CANADA

Distributed to the trade by The Ingram Book Company

Contents

Foreword

Dorothy Walker's book, *A Village in the Shadows*, is a welcome addition to the historiography of the Niagara Region. The story of St Davids has often been overlooked, eclipsed by the dramatic events that unfolded nearby at Queenston and in the Town of Niagara (Niagara-on-the-Lake).

Dorothy has meticulously gleaned what documents can be found covering the past 240 years in St Davids and has interviewed a number of residents descended from the original Loyalist settlers of the area, collecting family stories passed down through several generations. Some of these stories, undoubtedly embellished somewhat by time, are presented in a very interesting way to preserve the oral history of the village.

Today, driving through St Davids on the way to or from Niagara Falls, passing several heritage buildings surrounded by modern housing developments, it is easy to assume that this was simply a crossroads 150 years ago. *A Village in the Shadows* reveals it as a thriving village with industry, tradesmen and merchants and busy, loyal citizens.

Thanks to Dorothy Walker, a bright light has been shone on St Davids, and its colourful history has been brought out from under the shadows.

Ron Dale
Town of Niagara
2018

For the good people of St Davids—
past, present, and future.

Introduction 1

Writing a book on the history of a village is no easy task; writing about St Davids, a small community in the Niagara region of Ontario, Canada, was even more of a challenge. St Davids is a rural village surrounded by towns and cities that all have colourful histories of their own. To the north Niagara-on-the-Lake's "Old Town" offers visible evidence of the town's heritage and one only needs to walk a few steps to visit the Niagara Historical Museum. Historical plaques throughout the town provide excellent summaries of its proud history. St Davids lives in its shadow; it also lives in the shadow of the famous Niagara Falls to the south, Queenston to the east, and St. Catharines to the west. That is why this book is entitled *A Village in the Shadows*.

In 1776, a Declaration of Independence launched the birth of the American nation. Conflict had arisen when Great Britain attempted to assert economic control on her American colonies after a costly victory over the French during the Seven Years War. British attempts to impose taxes on the colonies resulted in protest and riots. The United Colonies of America wanted to become "free, and independent states," and American revolutionary colonists were ready to fight the British Parliament for it.[23]

Not all the population of the original thirteen colonies opposed Britain and, by 1779, many United Empire Loyalists flocked to Fort Niagara (on the east side of the Niagara River). They were an eclectic group of people— some were wealthy landowners and envied by the revolutionists who treated them atrociously. The hardships and danger during the journey to Canada were constant but hope for security was enormous.

In 1780, Lord Germain approved General Haldimand's proposal to reclaim land on the west side of the Niagara River granted by the Mississauga people to the British Crown and, in 1783, King George III signed a proclamation for land grants to be given to those who supported him.[51,74,75]

Although the hardships and miseries of frontier life were considerable, these determined people somehow coped; they built homes and toiled and struggled to forge a better life out of a rough country and were successful in that endeavour until June 18, 1812, when US president James Madison signed a declaration of war on Britain.

In 1803, Britain was engaged in the Napoleonic Wars and the Royal Navy was always short-handed. The Americans felt that the British were violating American sovereignty by seizing American seaman and enforcing an embargo against the French. War with Britain was a way to stop their arrogance, but to attack mainland England directly was impossible. Their only option was to invade its colony, Canada—and thus the senseless War of 1812-14 was declared. Neither side could proclaim a victory, and the loss of many lives caused devastation for American patriots, British Loyalists, and the Indigenous people. In the end, Loyalists and Republicans had to share the continent and learn to coexist.

The Niagara frontier bore the brunt of the hostilities. Descendants of Loyalist families still live in St Davids, and today at last have the security of which the early Loyalists only dreamed.

On November 9, 1789, Lord Dorchester declared that it was his wish to put the mark of honour upon the families who had adhered to the Unity of the Empire. Because of his statement, the printed militia rolls carried the notation:

> N.B. "*Those Loyalists who have adhered to the Unity of the Empire and joined the Royal Standard before the Treaty of Separation in the year 1783, and all their Children and their Descendants by either sex, are to be distinguished by the following Capitals, affixed to their names: U.E. Alluding to their great principle The Unity of the Empire."*

The initials "U.E." are rarely seen today, but the influence of the Loyalists on the evolution of Canada remains. Their ties with Britain and their antipathy to the United States provided the strength needed to keep Canada independent and distinct in North America.[23]

Introduction 2

BUTLER'S RANGERS, "INDIAN" ALLIES, AND MILITIA

The British Department of Indian Affairs was created to develop and maintain alliances with Indigenous nations. To maintain the alliance, the British frequently gave gifts of food, rum, blankets, cloth, clothing, tools, utensils, firearms, and ammunition to nations with whom they dealt. Most Indigenous nations living east of the Mississippi had become dependent on European-manufactured goods.

On September 15, 1777, John Butler was given orders to raise a battalion of Rangers to fight on behalf of the British against the American rebels. Some employees of the Indian Department became officers in the regiment, known as "Butler's Rangers." They were disbanded on June 24, 1784, and many Rangers settled with Loyalist land grants in the Niagara Peninsula.[21]

Indian Allies came mainly from the Six Nations Iroquois Confederacy. Many tribes initially pledged support to the British, while the Oneida and Tuscarora nations fought with the American rebels. Many others, particularly the Onondaga, chose to remain neutral. After the American Revolution, the Six Nations were given a large tract of land along the Grand River for the loss of their ancestral homelands in New York State.

The Nassau Militia—later called the Lincoln Militia, when the county name changed—was a military presence between 1788 and 1793. Men, mostly all volunteers, were expected to report for duty with their own firearm and a dark coat. In 1793, *The Militia Act* was passed in the second session of Upper Canada's First Legislature. Lieutenant Governor Simcoe's plan was to appoint lieutenants for each county who were empowered "to call out, arm, array, and train annually all males aged 16 to 50." Because the numbers were less than expected, the upper age was increased to 60 in 1794. Other provisions in the *Amending Act* required every man to provide himself with a "sufficient musket, fusil, rifle or gun with six rounds of ammunition," and to be available when called out for review exercise or actual service.[80,81]

A directive from the military secretary's office in Quebec, on January 2, 1813, states that uniforms approved for the militia of Upper Canada consist of a green jacket with red cuff and collar and white lace, blue "gunmouth" trousers, and felt regulation caps.[76]

Author's Note

As an English immigrant to Canada who lived for twenty years in Quebec, and who read extensively about the area when living in Singapore as a military wife and young mother, I have always had a fascination with southern Ontario. After moving from Quebec to English Canada in 1995, one day in early summer, my husband and I drove though St Davids on our way to Niagara-on-the-Lake, and it reminded me of the small English village where I spent my childhood. I felt the gentle ambience as we approached the four-way stop that defines the village and loved the leafy greenness of the rural setting. Little did we realize that, fifteen years later, we would retire here.

No book detailing the story of St Davids can ever be complete, and my only intention is to offer interesting information about the village and its vicinity. I hope you will catch my enthusiasm when I describe the history of the growing community and its fascinating past.

The book begins with a brief account of early history, and I have endeavoured to reflect the written word as accurately as available documents will allow. I have compiled information from many sources and included various quoted references. Sometimes, I have quoted from newspaper articles; they are rarely first-hand accounts, and therefore, I rely on the journalists and authors for the accuracy of their articles.

Many personal documents were lost in both the burning of Niagara and St Davids during the War of 1812; history has therefore left many questions unanswered. No doubt this book will be revised in future years to reflect newly discovered information.

During research, it became clear that the village was inextricably linked to its neighbours in the wider Niagara Peninsula. The American Revolution, the War of 1812, and the role of Indigenous nations all had a direct impact on St Davids and the early development of Canada. The reader will therefore find many descriptions of events that occurred outside the community.

The subject of how to address the unique Indigenous peoples I have written about, who lived and raised families in Canada and America before and after Europeans arrived, is often debated. When explorers arrived on the North American continent, they gave names to those first people when they could not pronounce those from their native language. The words "nation," "tribe," and "Indian" were in use in the period about which I have written and, in an effort not to offend any readers, I have taken care not to use the latter word unnecessarily. When I have used "Iroquois" and "Six Nations," it has been because many communities included people who retained distinct tribal characteristics outside the Iroquois Confederacy. If I have used the word "warrior," it has been because I acknowledge the pride of the people who served as fighters with British regulars or the militia, or as volunteers during that period of colonization, and they deserve recognition for their participation.

The village name, St Davids, can be seen to be spelled many ways. In this book, it is consistently spelled without a period in "St" and without an apostrophe in "Davids."

I have tried to avoid conjecture to make the story of our village as true as possible, and any inaccuracies should be minor. History is still unfolding, as St Davids assumes its role as a growing and thriving community in Niagara-on-the-Lake, Ontario. In the meantime, please enjoy reading about this unique community.

Mr. William Kirby's
"The Hungry Year"

"They who loved the cause that had been lost, and kept their faith
To England's Crown, and scorned an alien name
Passed into exile; leaving all behind except their honor, and the
Conscious pride
Of duty done to country and to King.
Broad lands, ancestral homes, the gathered wealth
Of patient toil and self-denying years
Were confiscate and lost
Not dropping like poor fugitives, they came
In exodus to our Canadian wilds,
But full of heart and hope, with heads erect and fearless eyes,
victorious in defeat.
With thousand toils, they forced their devious way
Through the great wilderness of silent woods
That gleamed o'er lake and stream, till higher rose
The northern star above the broad domain
Of half a continent, still theirs to hold,
Defend and keep forever as their own and England's to the end of
Time." [26,31]

In September 1839, William Kirby came to Niagara. He worked as a tanner for a time at St Davids. Later he became a schoolteacher, a novelist, and a poet. "The Hungry Year" was part of a collection of poems first published in the *Canadian Methodist Magazine* that was part of a series of poems named "Canadian Idylls." "The Hungry Year" tells the story of a drought on the Niagara frontier in 1788-89, which caused a poor harvest and severe food shortages for the United Empire Loyalists. [26]

1

ANCIENT NIAGARA RIVER

The sparkling blue water of the Niagara River shimmers and swirls in the bright sunshine on sunny days and turns the colour of green jade when the sun disappears on cloudy days. Either way, the river is beautiful. The village of St Davids is located approximately six kilometres west from its verge. The northerly flow of water from Lake Erie to Lake Ontario forms part of the border between the Province of Ontario in Canada, on the west side, and New York State in the United States, on the east side. It is fifty-eight kilometres long and includes Niagara Falls.[49]

To help us understand how St Davids came to exist, it is important to go back approximately 23,000 years, when the ancient Niagara River followed a path from the Whirlpool Rapids to where St Davids is today and emptied into the glacial Lake Iroquois; the escarpment being the shoreline of this ancient lake.

St Davids Gorge

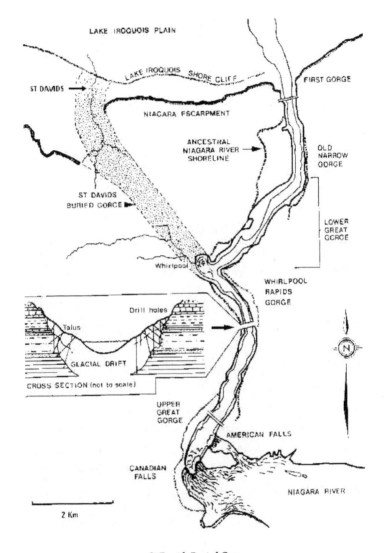

St Davids Buried Gorge
Courtesy: Niagara Falls Public Library

As the last glaciers retreated, the river gorge filled with debris, and when the glaciers completely melted, a new gorge was formed at the base of the escarpment where the community of Queenston is today. This became what is the present channel of the Niagara River. The ancient river gorge became known as St Davids Gorge,[48] and was the source of the cold-water spring that supplied Four Mile Creek and flowed down the valley through the village.

EUROPEAN MISSIONARIES

In the 1600s, many European missionaries passed by Niagara. One of them was the Flemish friar of the Recollet branch of the Order of St Francis, Father Hennepin (he came with explorer LaSalle)—one of the first known Europeans to set foot in the Niagara area. He wrote descriptions from his first knowledge of Niagara Falls. The Niagara shore periodically had been used by western fur traders portaging around Niagara Falls on well-beaten trails. Many years before the arrival of European missionaries and explorers, the Indigenous peoples had well-defined routes of travel that they used for hunting trips, and when they were on the warpath. They would follow the waterways wherever it was possible and use portage paths to avoid rapids.[1,37]

Louis Hennepin Sketch of Niagara Falls 1678
Courtesy: Library and Archives Canada

Thousands of years ago Niagara was settled by Native American people. In the early 1600s a community of Neutral Indians, Iroquoian-speaking Indigenous people, have been recorded as one of the earliest groups residing in the Niagara region. They claimed land on both sides of the Niagara River and the entire area was called Onguiaahra. Villages of the Neutrals were situated in forests not far away from the waterways, and a community of them lived along the banks of Four Mile Creek in St Davids, in the area north of where Stamford Townline Road is today.[38,49]

Onguiaahra means "the Strait" or "thundering waters" and is thought to be the origin of the word "Niagara." *The Niagara Township, Centennial History* describes another word, "Onyahrah," from the Iroquoian language, meaning "neck" or the strip of land between the two lakes.[1,49]

NEUTRAL PEOPLE

The Neutrals farmed the land and fished in the local waterways, which were teeming with brook trout, sturgeon, and salmon. The Neutral territory had Onondaga chert—microcrystalline quartz used in tools—near the eastern end of Lake Erie.[38,79] This valuable resource was used to make tools and projectiles e.g. spear-and arrowheads, which they supplied to their powerful neighbours, the Iroquois to the south (current-day New York State), and the Huron Nation to the north (central Ontario). Both tribes travelled back and forth across the peninsula as they regularly waged war against each other, but neither could claim complete victory. During these fierce battles, the Neutrals maintained a policy of neutrality and allowed both tribes to travel their territory without taking sides, while they continued to farm the rich Niagara soil. Their neutrality only applied to wars between the Huron and Iroquois, however; otherwise, they were anything but peaceful.

Around 1650, during a period now loosely referred to as the Beaver Wars, the Iroquois Confederacy wanted to dominate the fur trade with the Europeans by wiping out rivals who acted as middlemen between Indigenous peoples to the north and west who hunted and trapped furs for Europeans at Montreal and Albany; the Europeans would trade manufactured goods for those furs. The Seneca Nation had begun a series of attacks on neighbouring tribes in the 1640s, and the Five Nations annihilated the Petun, Wendat (Huron), Wenro, Erie, and Neutral nations. By 1653, the Neutrals had ceased to exist. Any who survived were incorporated mostly with the Seneca villages in New York, and assimilated into the Iroquois Confederacy, or were driven west to seek refuge among other Indigenous nations. With the demise of the Neutral Nation, the Niagara Peninsula had few Indigenous people until the Mississaugas (Anishinaabe)[38] moved into the area, seizing the land from the Seneca. It was the Mississaugas Nation who were using the Niagara area as hunting grounds when the first settlers began to arrive in the 1770s.[38]

OSSUARY

An "Indian" burial ground was found in 1828, south of St Davids, and west of the stone cairn on St. Paul Avenue on the top of the Niagara Escarpment. Many bodies were found there, in one long grave. Clay pipes, trinkets, pottery, beads, and bear claws were discovered with them, and given to the Royal Ontario Museum. Other artifacts were sold to interests in Buffalo and western New York State. A stone cairn with a carved arrow-head marks the burying ground. A dedication ceremony in St Davids took place in 1934.[5,10]

Dedication of Ossuary commemorative cairn 1934
Courtesy: Niagara Falls Public Library

FORT NIAGARA

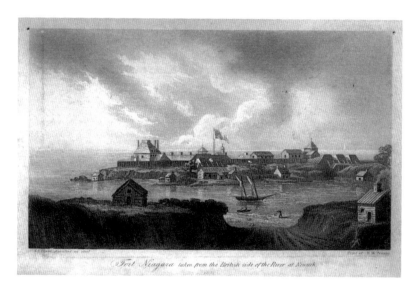

Fort Niagara 1814: Joseph Ives Pease
Courtesy: Toronto Public Library

During the colonial wars in North America, a fort at the mouth of the Niagara River was fundamental to controlling access to the upper Great Lakes, and to the route west to the centre of the continent. The fort was also extremely important as a base for diplomacy with the different "Indian" tribes. Fort Niagara was also the command centre and link to the routes of military communication and supply with other frontier outposts, including Detroit and Michilimackinac.[43,78]

In 1726, on the east side of the river, opposite what is today Niagara-on-the-Lake, the French military erected Fort Niagara, a permanent fortification surrounding a substantial stone building that resembled a beautiful French castle. Possession of the fort would be a great strategic advantage for the British and, in 1759, British regulars, colonial soldiers, and Six Nation allies mounted an attack against the fort. After a nineteen-day siege, the French surrendered and withdrew from the Niagara Peninsula. Fort Niagara immediately became central to Britain's communication with its military resources, providing a suitable storehouse for supplies, and trading for goods to be dispatched to the other frontier forts on the Great Lakes. It also became a key centre for the British Indian Department, the organization responsible for developing and maintaining alliances with Indigenous nations.[78]

In 1765, on the west bank of the river opposite Fort Niagara, the British constructed a log building and named it "Navy Hall." It was used as a military complex, supply store, and naval base.

AMERICAN REVOLUTION

Eleven years later, in 1776, a declaration of independence was approved by the Continental Congress. American colonists revolted against the British government, declaring that the United Colonies wanted to be free and independent states.[3] This action triggered the American Revolution, which changed the landscape of North America.

In the days, months, and years that followed, political turmoil and social upheaval were widespread. As with modern-day warfare, people were displaced, resulting in native and Loyalist families being forced from their homes in the Mohawk Valley (New York State), and escaping to Fort Niagara in multitudes. The refugees included those who had German, Dutch, Swiss, and English backgrounds. The flourishing villages and orchards of the Seneca and Cayuga Nations had been levelled to the ground by the Sullivan-Clinton Campaign,[41,43] and the displaced Iroquois families fled to Fort Niagara, with little more than the barest essentials, to camp outside on land that extended approximately six miles south.

Later, the Mohawk, Onondaga, Cayuga, and Seneca of the Six Nations, who had been allies of the British, were incredibly distressed when they discovered that the Treaty of Paris of 1783 had been agreed to without any regard for their land needs.[89] They could not understand how the king of England could surrender their recognized territories, which did not belong to him. The Oneida and the Tuscarora, the other two tribes of the Six Nations, were allied with the American rebels during the war.

Lieutenant Colonel Mason Bolton, who commanded the garrison of Fort Niagara, did his best with the meagre supplies on hand to support the substantial number of refugees, including the Indigenous people who put an enormous strain on the food supplies. Also, the lack of proper medicine at the garrison contributed to many deaths. In response to this concern, General Frederick Haldimand, Governor of Canada and commander of British forces, in a letter dated September 13, 1779,[51] recommended a farming and resettlement program that could take place only after the severe winter turned to spring the following year. He gave permission for selected families to move to the west bank of the Niagara River to settle on land acquired by the Crown from the Mississauga people. Priority was given to wounded and older Butler's Rangers who had been released from active duty—e.g., individuals considered unable to continue active service, and civilian refugees who had gathered at Fort Niagara.[16,43]

These refugees had a direct impact on both the development of the Niagara Peninsula and the establishment of St Davids.

3

Refugees

As one drives around the prosperous Niagara Peninsula today, the abundance of flourishing farms, orchards, and vineyards makes it difficult to imagine how it must have been in the late 1700s, when refugees descended on Fort Niagara. By 1779, the garrison had become a fully developed outpost as a trade and supply depot, and military headquarters for soldiers and sailors—a diplomatic centre with Indian Department agents (Butler's Rangers used it as a staging ground), interpreters, blacksmiths and other traders, and their families.

The progression of the American Revolution had become unstoppable, and many colonists of the thirteen colonies were adamant about rejecting the authority of the British Parliament. The Crown wanted to impose taxation on them, and was passing laws without colonial representation, which the colonists considered illegal under the 1689 British Bill of Rights.[56]

Not all the colonists opposed Britain. There were many who remained loyal to King George III, including some Indigenous people who also supported him. Despite the loss of their homes, farms, businesses, and way of life, they felt a deep desire to live with the orderly laws and security they had known under the British Crown in pre-revolutionary times; a continuation of this type of government was now being promised in Canada. The colonies they left proved not to be a place to set down long-term roots, and, in desperation, they had braved the long, arduous journey to seek refuge at Fort Niagara.

Their journey would most likely have been on foot or in two-horse wagons, or even one-horse conveyances, and perhaps ox carts along "Indian" trails and woodland tracks. Some came by the Hudson River to Oswego and crossed Lake Ontario by bateaux, canoes, or sailing vessels. Whichever way they journeyed to the fort, they must have felt enormous relief, and perhaps were encouraged by the respect and compassion shown by the British authorities. The lack of shelter and shortage of essential supplies within and around the garrison was a huge problem that caused a great strain on the fort's resources. Illness and disease were apparent everywhere, especially among the young and elderly. Yet as terrible as the situation was, these desperate people could only have felt optimistic in hearing that land was opening for settlement on the west bank of the Niagara River. To make a new life and endure the enormous challenge of creating farms and homesteads out of virgin land beyond the immediate area of Navy Hall and the military complex and supply store, they had to be resilient.

RESETTLEMENT

Lord Germain approved General Haldimand's farming/resettlement program for Loyalist families to raise grain and cattle in the Niagara vicinity to supply the fort, so that troops and Indigenous refugees could be fed.[51] In a letter to Lieutenant Colonel Bolton, dated July 7, 1780, he stated "he will reclaim the land on the southwest of the river, opposite the fort granted by the Mississaugas to Sir William Johnson for the Crown in 1764.[40,77] Lands are to be divided into several lots and distributed to such Loyalists who can improve them."

His letter also clearly stated: "Those who settle on the land are not to consider that they have the smallest right to any part thereof, the produce alone excepted (sic) being their property. They will hold their possessions from year to year, which will be granted to them, by the Commander-in-Chief for the time being as their property according to their merits. If at any time they should remove, either from inclination or by order of the commanding officer, they are to have permission to dispose of their crops, stock of cattle, etc., and a reasonable allowance will be made to them for their improvements; for their further encouragement, no rent will be required of them. Provisions such as seed, grain, ploughs, and other implements would be provided by the government; however, it was made clear that any produce from the farms, over and above what was needed for their own consumption, was to be sold to the Commanding Officer at the fort for the use of the troops, and not to traders or passing travellers."[51]

Lieutenant Colonel Butler was tasked with settling families from within his corps. Priority was given to soldiers who were too old or not healthy enough to withstand the constant rigours of Butler's campaign. It was important to Haldimand's plan that the settlers have farming experience.

LOYALIST FAMILIES

General Haldimand requested that John Butler prepare a survey of west Niagara, and, on August 25, 1780, he reported that sixteen families, totalling sixty-eight people, had settled. These early settlers included Peter Secord, John Secord, James Secord, Isaac Dolson, George Stuart, George Fields, John Depue, Daniel Rowe, Elijah Phelps, Philip Bender, Samuel Lutz, Michael Showers, Hemanus House, Thomas McMicking, Adam Young, and McGregor Van Every. These families were settled without clear title to any land, or lease or security of their farms.[31,51]

ST. DAVIDS & VICINITY

Ottawa Archives Map No. 25 - 1784

Sheubel Welton Papers

Excerpts from Niagara Township

Glebe ¹²⁹	Jno. Clement ¹⁰²	83	John Clement ⁵⁶	A. Cumings ³⁷ ham, George Dowdig? R. Vrooman
Glebe ¹³⁰	Adam Crysler ¹⁰¹	Joseph ⁸⁴ Brown	Solomon ⁵⁵ Quick	Jas. ³⁶ Durham
Adam ¹³¹ Crysler	Adam Crysler ¹⁰⁰	Adam ⁸⁵ Crysler	Adam ⁵⁴ Crysler	Charles ³⁹ Dupuis
Joseph ¹³² Page	Adam Crysler ⁹⁹	John ⁸⁶ Crysler	Stephen ⁵³ Secord	Peter ⁴⁰ Miller
Joseph ¹³³ Page	Jno. Turney ⁹⁸	87	Stephen ⁵² Secord	Stephen ⁴¹ Secord
Joseph ¹³⁴ Page	Jno. Turney ⁹⁷	Samson ⁸⁸ Lutes	Col. J. ⁵¹ Butler	David ⁴² Secord
Christian ¹³⁵ Warner	Samuel Lutes ⁹⁶	Samson ⁸⁹ Lutes ST.DAVIDS	David ⁵⁰ Secord	David ⁴³ Secord
Christian ¹³⁶ Warner	95	Peter ⁹⁰ Secord	Stephen ⁴⁹ Secord	Samuel ⁴⁴ Street
Christian ¹³⁷ Warner	94	Peter ⁹¹ Secord	Stephen ⁴⁸ Secord	Samuel ⁴³ Street
Christian ¹³⁸ Warner	93	Peter ⁹² Secord	David ⁴⁷ Secord	Conrad ⁴⁶ Duchman
6th Conc.	5th Conc.	4 mile Creek	3rd Conc.	2nd Conc.

25

NIAGARA Township No 1.

Niagara Historical Society, Niagara on the Lake; Vol 41, *Records of Niagara, A Collection of Contemporary Letters and Documents 1790-1792.* Collected and Edited by Brig. General E. A. Cruickshank, 1930.
(NOTE: REVERSED MAP , Lake Ontario is NORTH of the Township..
ALSO: This map previously attributed to the year 1784, but is likely later than 1800.)]

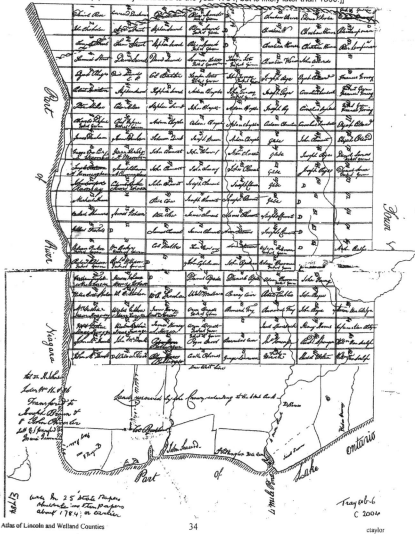

Atlas of Lincoln and Welland Counties   34   ctaylor

Notes

Top row, 4th column: Lots 90, 91 and 92 indicate allocation to Peter Secord.

Columns 6 and 7: Lots 135, 138, 140, 141, 150 and 151 indicate allocation to Christian Warner.

Far right (column 8): Lots 178, 179 and 180 indicate allocation to Francis Goring.

PETER SECORD (1726-1818)

In August 1780, Peter, aged fifty-three, was discharged from active military service, and he and his second wife, Abigail, were given permission to cross to the west bank of the river with five of his thirteen children (listed in the 1782 census of Niagara). They had brought with them five horses and were given approval to begin clearing and preparing the land for farming in the area that was destined to become St Davids.

At the beginning of the American Revolution, Peter Secord and two of his brothers had joined the Butler's Rangers—Peter, a sergeant; James, a lieutenant; and John, a private. These brothers were the great-grandchildren of Ambroise Sicard, who had arrived in New York from France via England in 1681. Most of the Secord families in southwestern Ontario are descended from these three Rangers.[22]

Peter, clearly a man of action, gained permission from the new commandant of Niagara, Brigadier General Powell, to survey land at his own expense, and although he did not have ownership, he settled on Lots 90, 91, and 92. Totalling 300 acres, these lots straddled both sides of Four Mile Creek, below the escarpment south of York Road, which today is the centre of St Davids. Later, another grant of 400 acres was given to Peter at Long Point Settlement in Norfolk County.[22]

Clearing dense forest and constructing buildings was an enormous task for Peter and his family, and owning both a sawmill and gristmill would be advantageous, but he did not own the land and needed government permission. This was refused, but the need for the mills was acknowledged, and Lieutenant David Brass of the Butler's Rangers was commissioned to do the work.

"Butler was instructed that the Government would bear the cost of the construction for the mills and the Secord family would be allowed to work them in accordance with the seigniorial custom of the province as 'banal' [common] mills,[74] which the farmers would be obliged to use for grinding grain and sawing timber." In 1783, both mills were built south of York Road. For the next ten years, Peter and his family worked on the property. Even though he made many petitions to the government, the land was not awarded to Peter until 1798, by which time he had left the area to settle in Norfolk County. In 1799, Peter granted ownership of his land to David Secord Jr. Shortly thereafter, David granted the land to David Secord Sr. (later known as Major David), son of James Secord.[22, 25]

The sawmill operated until it was destroyed by fire during the burning of St Davids in 1814. The gristmill fortunately survived, and today it is a private home. The community at that time was called Four Mile Mills.

JAMES SECORD (1732-1784)

James, a brother of Peter Secord, was born in New Rochelle, Westchester County, New York. He married Madelaine Badeau, and, in 1777, he joined the Butler's Rangers. In 1780, he led fifty-four of his neighbours and three sons to Fort Niagara. He and his family crossed the Niagara River to what is now Queenston at the same time as brother Peter. In 1780, James received permission from Colonel Mason Bolton to settle with his wife and seven children on 300 acres of land at Queenston Landing. In 1782, Butler's first census of Niagara reports that James had cleared twenty acres and produced crops of corn, potatoes, and wheat. Little else is known of James, other than that he was the father of Major David Secord and James Secord, husband of Laura Ingersoll. James died at Queenston on July 13, 1784. His will distributed land to sons David (age twenty-five) and James (age eleven).[22]

DAVID SECORD (1759-1844)

David, son of James Secord and Madelaine Badeau, married three times and sired fourteen children. In 1777, he joined the Butler's Rangers and served as a sergeant until 1784. After the war, he became very successful in business and was known as "King David," an honorific given to leading businessmen. He was very instrumental in how St Davids evolved.

Apart from his business success, David became a magistrate in 1796, and, in 1809, he was elected to the fifth parliament of Upper Canada, representing 2nd Lincoln. He also served in the 2nd Lincoln Militia,[82] and reached the rank of major in 1806. He claimed to have fought in every significant engagement in the Niagara district during the War of 1812. He commanded a regiment at the battle of Lundy's Lane in 1814. During the burning of St Davids in July 1814, his buildings, later valued at £3,796, were destroyed. Between the years of 1817 and 1820, David sat in the House of Assembly for 3rd Lincoln in the seventh parliament. He lived a comfortable life until his death at age eighty-five.[22]

JAMES SECORD JR. (1773-1841)

James, son of James Secord Sr., younger brother of David, would have been seven years old when his father crossed the Niagara River. When he was old enough, he joined the 1st Lincoln Militia, and later served as a wagon driver in the Car Brigade,[82] under Isaac Swayze, in 1812. The same day that Brock was killed at Queenston Heights, James was badly wounded in the knee and shoulder. He later recovered from his injuries, but lived with pain for the rest of his life. After the war, he became a customs collector and lived with his wife, Laura, in Chippawa until 1841, when he died of a stroke.[22]

CHRISTIAN WARNER (1754-1833)

Christian was the only son and heir of Michael Warner, of Lutheran Swiss nationality, who arrived in the American colonies in 1739. Christian lived near Albany when the revolution broke out. In 1778, he joined the Butler's Rangers and served as a sergeant until 1784. Christian and his wife, Charity Gertrude Eckert, also from Albany, were married in New York Province in 1775, and had twelve children. In November 1812, a married daughter died (cause unknown). Four other children died in 1814—two girls, Kesia and Catherine, were victims of cholera; Michael died of exposure after lending his blanket to a comrade. Although inscriptions are unclear due to the ravage of time, a row of headstones is present on the burial ground on Warner Road, close to the Queen Elizabeth Way (QEW).

An article by Jean Huggins in 1978 describes the Warner family: "Christian Warner and family (wife and two small children) crossed the Niagara River somewhere between 1783 and 1784 (the exact date cannot be established). It is recorded that the children were carried in baskets across the back of a cow. Before provisions were supplied by the government, a cow, an axe, and an auger were priceless possessions. Records indicate that the Warner name was on the provisions list in 1786; a family of six is recorded." The family settled on Lots 135-138, just below the mountain and west of St Davids. Their first dwelling, a log cabin, was shortly replaced by a rough-cast house. This was burned in the 1870s and another was built in its place.[12]

Sometime after they arrived, Christian became a passionate Methodist and was known for his "power" in prayer. He held meetings on his property, half a mile from his home in a nook in the dense forest, and his sermons could be heard two miles away. It is not known when he first started to lead prayer sessions, but they continued for forty-five years. He was very strict about dressing simply; he did not approve of men wearing suspenders, nor women wearing frilly caps. In later years, he gained excessive weight and needed support to hold up his trousers, but refused to have more than one suspender. Christian was very much respected by his fellow citizens, and, as a neighbour, he was kind and obliging and much loved during his life. He died in 1833.[45,67]

The Warner meeting house continued to hold meetings until 1870, when it was replaced with a smaller building. In 1908, the building was sold at a public auction to Hudson Usher and Edwin David Lowrey.

CLEMENT FAMILY

Three Clement brothers settled in and around St Davids, and all sired large families. John and James took Crown land below the ridge and Joseph settled in St Davids.

JOSEPH CLEMENT (1750-1812)

Joseph Clement, first son of Ludovicus (Lewis) Cobes Clement and Eliza Poutman, was born in Tryon County, New York. Like his father, Joseph served as a lieutenant in the Indian Department, and became a Butler's Ranger during the Revolutionary War. In 1783, he lived in Montreal, where he met Mary Margaret Duffet (1766-1845). Mary was born during the French regime and educated at Hotel Dieu Nunnery. Her father had been a surgeon in the French military, and he disapproved of Joseph's interest in Mary, who was sixteen years younger. In that era, doctors made medical visits on horseback, and whenever that happened, a letter was concealed in the padded part of Dr. Duffet's saddle and an answer was returned the same way. These letters resulted in an elopement—Joseph and Mary married on May 9, 1784.

For Joseph's service to the British, he received a town lot in Niagara and 1,600 acres of land in the Township of Binbrook, which enabled him to build great wealth. Mary and Joseph settled in St Davids and brought up six daughters and four sons there. Joseph is credited with being among the first freemasons under the seal of Lodge No. 56 in the Kings or 8th Regiment of Foot in 1780 at Niagara.[68]

In 1812, he mysteriously disappeared, and because no body was found, there has been speculation over the years that he had been the victim of a dreaded terminal disease (possibly cancer). Not wanting to be a burden to his family, he put his affairs in order, made his will, and took his own life. Suicide being a great disgrace, the family kept the secret and buried his body under the floor of his barn. When the search for his body ended, they reburied him in the family plot. Although no tombstone shows his place of birth, it is believed that he was buried with Mary, where her headstone lies in the Warner burial ground. There is a three-foot wall surrounding Mary's tombstone, which includes son Richard and daughter Jemima, and three small stones that are unreadable. Attached to the outside of the wall close to Mary's grave is a bronze plaque dedicated to Joseph. It is believed that the true facts of Joseph's death have been known to the Woodruff and Clement families for the last 200 years.[34,68]

JOHN PUTNAM CLEMENT (1759-1845)

John Clement, (Ranger John) served as a lieutenant in the Indian Department. He was the second son of Lewis Cobes. He first married Margaret Crysler, daughter of Adam Crysler and Ann Brown, around 1779. Margaret was born in 1761 and died around 1781; there is no record of her coming to Canada. His second marriage was to Mary Ball, in 1786. They had thirteen children. Mary died in their home on Lot 103 in Niagara from an unknown cause in 1858. She is buried in St. Marks Church cemetery beside her husband's grave.

In 1794 Lieutenant Colonel John Butler, County of Lincoln, com-
missioned John Clement to be Captain of militia forces, raised within the
County of Lincoln.[64] Robert's History of Freemasonry[68] discloses that in the
War of 1812-1814, during the fighting at Chippawa, John saved the life of a
captured American who was about to be scalped by one of the Indian allies.
Some months later John, himself, was captured and imprisoned in New York
State, where he discovered that his overseer was the same man whose life he
had saved. Out of appreciation for sparing his life, his ex-prisoner arranged
for John to escape and provided him with a horse and wagon to take him to
the frontier.[68]

JAMES CLEMENT (1764-1813)

James Clement, third son of Lewis Cobes, was born in Mohawk Valley,
New York. James was an ensign in the Indian Department during the latter part of the Revolutionary War. He married Catherine Crysler in 1786
and received a 2,000-acre land grant in Niagara Township, and a town lot
in Niagara. In 1794 Lieutenant Colonel John Butler, County of Lincoln,
commissioned James to be a Lieutenant of militia forces, raised within the
County of Lincoln.

During the War of 1812, James was a dispatch carrier between Niagara
and Fort Erie. On March 3, 1813, he sustained an injury to his hand, and
four months later he died of sepsis. On July 13, Catherine died giving birth
to a daughter, and her baby also died. James, Catherine, and their daughter
are buried together on Lot 103 on the south side of Line 6, just west of Four
Mile Creek Road. Legend has it that the home was spared from being burned
by retreating American soldiers because Catherine was a widow, pregnant,
and living alone with her many children. The deaths of James and Catherine
left their eldest son Joseph the responsibility of bringing up his siblings.[68]

TEUNIS (ANTHONY) SLINGERLAND (1723-1794)

Anthony, an officer of Adam Vrooman's Company (Albany Battalion Division), married Clartje Clute. His lands were plundered and looted by rebels
so, for safety, he brought his wife, four sons, and daughter to Canada in 1783.
Three of his sons served under Colonel Butler in the Ranger's Corps. In

1792, Anthony petitioned for a land grant and received 120 acres in Niagara. He died in 1794, and is buried at St. Mark's Church.

An Anthony Jr. and Sr., likely both a son and grandson of Teunis Anthony, appear on the muster of rolls of Captain J. C. Ball's Company of the 1ˢᵗ Regiment of Lincoln Militia dated June 5, 1820 (RG.C1702, P.49), Public Archives of Canada. Later descendants of Teunis Anthony (Howard and son Donald Slingerland) lived for many years in St Davids; Howard was a successful businessman in the village. More information on the Slingerland family can be found in Chapter 19.

These indomitable settlers were determined to stay loyal to King George III. They began a new way of life and adapted to their new environment. The immediate clearing of land was crucial to start the process for planting crops to feed themselves. Building a home was equally important. This was done by felling trees. The walls were built of logs. Gaps were filled with wood chips and sealed with mud. The roof was possibly covered with overlapping pieces of bark. Doors were made of pieces of timber slit into rough boards. In some cases, door hinges and latches were made of wood.[70] These dwellings would have included a fireplace for cooking, and a favourite place for sleeping. Fresh fish from the Niagara River and Four Mile Creek were part of the settlers' diet, along with quail, rabbit, duck, and wild turkey.[1]

During the late 1780s and early 1790s, the promise of land settlements by the British government attracted a wave of immigrants from the newly formed United States. In addition to being enticed by the available land, these immigrants were reacting to post-revolution political upheaval and economic challenges. The British provided them with 200 acres of land, but not the tools and provisions they had given to the earlier Loyalists.[32]

1795 Onward

EZEKIEL WOODRUFF (1763-1837)[29] was the tenth of eleven children of Nathanial Woodruff and Mary Kilbourn, of Farmington, Connecticut. It is said that he served as an adjutant in the Revolutionary Army during the latter part of the war, but resigned in 1782, before his marriage to Sarah Hall (the sixth child of Captain Giles and Anna [Lord] Hall). Ezekiel was highly educated. He studied law at Yale University and began a practice in Litchfield and then Middletown, Connecticut. After the war, dissatisfied with the bitter struggle for self-government in America, he decided he wanted the protection of the Crown, despite the fact he had fought against it. In July 1795, at age thirty-two, he travelled with his family of five children (the eldest being only twelve) to Newark (previously called Niagara) to obtain a land grant; this would have required a swearing of loyalty to the Crown.

He quickly discovered that this new land was a wilderness with small settlements and few amenities. He found that it was not possible to practice law in Canada, so he began teaching, which did not pay well. In his spare time, he took up surveying, which was in great demand because of the rapid growth of communities. Within two years, he applied for and received land grants in Walpole and Wainfleet that totalled 600 acres.

During the following decade, his family increased to five sons and two daughters. Two of his sons became leading businessmen and both married into the Loyalist Clement family.[29]

RICHARD WOODRUFF (1784-1872), the second child of Eze-

kiel, came with his family to Newark in 1795. He married Ann Clement, daughter of Joseph Clement and Mary Duffet. The Woodruff family were educated, business-minded, and socially connected in the community. They were very influential in the growth of St Davids, and accumulated much of their fortune through land dealings.

In 1812, Richard would have been twenty-eight years old. He was a sergeant in the Niagara Light Dragoons [71,82] and served in Brock's force at the capture of Detroit.[29,71] Richard received a campaign medal for his participation in that event. He became an ensign in the 1st Lincoln Militia.[82] Being a war veteran, he was granted 200 acres of land. Land Registry Document #5140—appendix D—St Davids (Lot 90) indicates that a piece of land may have been bought from David Secord in 1811, but not registered until April 1817. During the tragic burning of St Davids in 1814, his home and family store were both destroyed by US soldiers. Records show that, in 1826, David Secord sold one-and-a-half acres of land on Lot 90 in St Davids to Richard.

Following the war, Richard worked in partnership with his younger brother William. Together, they managed a store and built and operated the first steam-powered gristmill in the village.[29]

Later, Richard was elected to the Assembly of Upper Canada and served as representative for the first riding of Lincoln in the 13th Assembly of Upper Canada in 1837. He became a justice of the peace in 1833. Richard died in 1872.[29]

WILLIAM WOODRUFF (1793-1860),[29] the fifth child of Ezekiel,

was born in Middleton, Connecticut, and married Margaret Clement. William's career was like that of his brother Richard. He served as a private in Crooks' Company at the beginning of the War of 1812. He was under Captain McClellan at the Battle of Queenston Heights. He was promoted to ensign in the 1st Regiment of the Lincoln Militia in 1815, and to lieutenant in August 1824. Like Richard, he was awarded a land grant of 200 acres.

Following the war in 1815, he entered into a partnership with Richard and together they operated the steam mill and general store in St Davids. The house that had been destroyed in 1814 (at the corner of Warner Road and Four Mile Creek Road) was rebuilt and became the home of William. William took a prominent part in public affairs, and was elected a member of the Assembly of Upper Canada, serving in the 10th Parliament under Sir John Colborne as the representative for the 1st and 2nd Ridings of Lincoln County. He served for two sessions (1829 and 1830). He also served as clerk of Niagara Township from 1820-1822. He was a magistrate at St Davids from 1828-1830, and was also appointed by the government as one of the directors of the Welland Canal.[29]

With the signing of the Paris Treaty ending the revolution in April 1783, and the purchase of land from the Mississauga people in 1784, more families settled along the west bank of the Niagara River. From then until 1812, the Niagara Peninsula became more established, and St Davids became an important milling centre using waters from Four Mile Creek. Homes and businesses were built, and the lives of the settlers improved.

4

Naming a Village

It is intriguing to know how the settlement of St Davids was named. Peter Secord and family members settled in the area from 1780 onward. Two Secord mills were built around 1783, when the community was known as Four Mile Mills. Afterward, local people began calling the village Davidsville and Davidstown.

In later years, Peter's nephew David Secord provided leadership and the nickname "King David" was given to him by those who lived here. However, it is generally accepted that Richard "King Dick" Woodruff founded the community in the 1800s.

During an interview with fifth-generation Richard Woodruff, he stated that, "after 1800, the village was named after David Secord." David was a major in the 2nd Militia while Richard's ancestor was a sergeant in the Niagara Light Dragoons.[71,82] "King Dick" named the village after his friend and superior officer. Later, the accepted name David somehow transmuted into St Davids, with an "s." It is still not clear how the "St" was added.

The *Mitchell & Co.'s General Directory for the Town of St Catharines and Gazetteer of the Counties of Lincoln and Welland for 1865*[39] states that "St Davids was a small post village situated in the township of Niagara, and county of Lincoln, on Four-[mile] Creek, within one mile of the Great Western railway,[83] and the same distance from the Erie and Niagara Railway. The first settlement was made in the year 1800, by Richard Woodruff; and the village was laid out by John Cassalman. The post office was established in 1858, with James C. Woodruff as postmaster, who was succeeded by Charles

Fisher. Four Mile Creek gives excellent facilities for manufacturing. There are two mills situated on it, containing two run of stones each, besides a tannery, all in successful operation. The village also contains two general stores; one hotel; one common school with average attendance of forty pupils; and one church built of frame, seated for 250 persons and used in common by all denominations. Mail daily, population about 300."

5

War of 1812

After the American Revolutionary War ended, the Niagara Peninsula thrived. Land continued to be surveyed and granted to settlers as they continued to arrive on the west bank of the river. By 1810, relations between Britain and the United States had grown steadily worse, and the threat of another war hung all along the frontier, like thunder clouds building up on the horizon before a storm. Everyone felt the increasing sound of war drums, especially farmers and settlers along the border who lived in fear and anticipation that the Americans might come at any time, including under cover of darkness. General Brock's intuition pushed him to build and train a Canadian militia, and to increase fortifications along the border. His intuition was correct, and, on June 18, 1812, the United States Congress and Senate declared war against Great Britain.

In his book, *The Good Soldier,* Canadian military historian D. J. Goodspeed mentions that Brock became aware of the declaration of war as early as June 25 from a messenger of Thomas Clark of Queenston (a local agent for the John Jacob Astor fur-trading company of New York).[17] Brock wasted no time. On August 6, together with his regular troops and militia volunteers, including his Provincial Aide de Camp John Macdonell, he travelled to Amherstburg. There, he met his "Indian" allies, who introduced him to the Shawnee chief, Tecumseh. Despite Brock's small number of troops, Tecumseh and his warriors pledged their help, and agreed to Brock's plan to take Fort Detroit. Brock marched his small army to Sandwich, (now part of Windsor) and, with a cool head, delivered a summons for American commander General Hull to surrender. Having read captured letters of General Hull, Brock played on his fear of an "Indian massacre." He planned to scare him into believing that he commanded many more troops than he did, including "a numerous body of Native warriors who have attached themselves to my troops."[17,61] Hull refused, and British guns at Sandwich began firing at Detroit. Hull's guns returned fire, but neither side inflicted much damage. During the night of August 15, several hundred Indians crossed the Detroit River. Early the next morning, Brock also crossed the river with his small army of regulars and militia and, marched toward the fort. Before attacking the fort, Brock sent a second message to Hull, again demanding surrender. This time, Hull succumbed to his fear of "Indian" brutality, and surrendered by raising a white flag.[61,62]

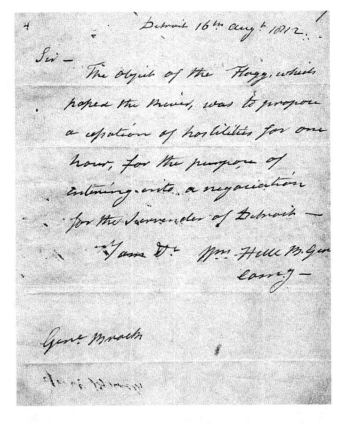

Brig. Gen. Hull's surrender letter to Maj. Gen. Brock

On August 16, 1812, Brock wrote a dispatch to Sir George Prevost informing him of the capture of Fort Detroit "without the sacrifice of a drop of British blood."[63] The frontier was now safe for the time being, and Brock was anxious to return to the Niagara River, where another American army was amassing for invasion.[17]

This invasion was to come before dawn on October 13, when American troops crossed the Niagara River and began invading Queenston Heights.[17]

During an historic attempt to defend Canadian soil, General Brock was hit in the chest by an American bullet. He collapsed and died, and his devastated troops carried his body from the battlefield. With the death of Brock, leadership fell to General Sheaffe, who was Brock's second-in command. Mid-afternoon the same day, General Sheaffe, and six companies of militia, British Regulars, and First Nation Warriors, plus a company of Black volunteers from Lincoln and York counties, scaled the escarpment east of St Davids (a

Surrender of Fort Detroit

Battle of Queenston Heights: John David Kelly
Courtesy: Library and Archives Canada

stone marker can be found on York Road) and managed to overcome the American invaders.

In May 1813, American ships began to bombard Fort George, and shortly thereafter an American force landed, captured, and occupied the length of the Niagara River between Niagara and Fort Erie until December 10, 1813.

St Davids was held by the Americans six times and the British seven times. In between, there were periods when it was virtually a "no man's land." After the wanton burning and destruction of Niagara, today known as Niagara-on-the-Lake, by the retreating American army on December 10, 1813, 400 people were rendered homeless and all public buildings, including the jail-house and library, were destroyed. After the British reoccupied Niagara and the ruins of Fort George, Major General de Rottenburg, the military and civilian commander of Upper Canada, established his headquarters at St Davids.[61] On December 16, Lieutenant General Drummond replaced de Rottenburg and took over civil and military command.[62] Temporarily, St Davids became the headquarters of the British Army in Upper Canada. In St Davids, Drummond and Colonel John Murray masterminded a plan for the capture of Fort Niagara.[1]

Drummond issued orders from Solomon Quick's Tavern (on what is now Paxton Lane, across from St Davids Golf Course) to Colonel John Murray to mobilize over 500 troops. They crossed the river and proceeded to Fort Niagara. It was no easy target, but at five in the morning of December 19, 1813, just before daylight, and after a short but severe interaction with very little loss of British lives, Fort Niagara was captured.[33,78] A shot was fired from the fort to the west Niagara shore indicating victory to Major General Phineas Riall, who was waiting for the signal to mobilize his troops to invade Lewiston. Lewiston was destroyed along with other settlements along the Niagara River, including Buffalo. Every building was reduced to ashes in retaliation for the abominable act of burning the town of Niagara.[57]

THE BURNING OF ST DAVIDS

Early in the morning on July 3, 1814, Americans landed at Fort Erie, and American Major General Jacob Brown's army forced the garrison and its commander to surrender. The next day, the Americans advanced toward Chippawa as the retreating British were firing and destroying bridges at each creek in the hope of delaying the Americans advance to the Chippawa (Welland) River. In the ensuing battle of Chippawa, the British forces under the command of Major General Riall endured heavy losses. They withdrew across the river. Two days later, Riall moved back even further as the Americans crossed the river, advanced to Queenston, and occupied it.[61,62]

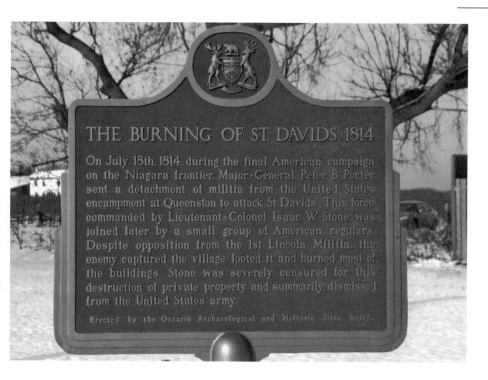

St Davids commemorative plaque
Photograph courtesy: John Donald Foley

On July 19, 1814, under the command of Colonel Isaac Stone, the plundering, looting, and deliberate burning of St Davids by American militia was a tragedy. Following victories at Fort Erie and Chippawa, the Americans proceeded north and established their camp at Queenston. British troops were based at Fort George. Clashes between the two armies were frequent, and one attempt resulted in trying to disperse Canadian militia near St Davids who were frustrating American reconnoitering parties.

A letter from Major Daniel McFarland (23rd US Infantry at Queenston) to his wife, dated July 1814, is revealing: "The whole population is against us, not encamped, a foraging party but is fired on and not infrequently returns with missing numbers. The militia have burnt several private dwellings and on the 19th (July) burnt in St Davids 30-40 homes."[6]

Close to St Davids on July 18, a small detachment of Lincoln militia surprised some American scouts west of the village. In the skirmish, the horse of US Commanding Officer Colonel Isaac Stone was killed.[14] His furious revenge came on July 19, when he gave orders to burn St Davids. Colonel Stone's men plundered and looted everything they could find, setting fire to dwellings as they left. The inhabitants said the burning was deliberate, undertaken to prevent the British from ever using it as their headquarters again. Later in a letter, Colonel Stone said that the burning had been accidental, and that he did not order the village to be put to the torch. He was subsequently dismissed in disgrace by General Jacob Brown for having acted contrary to orders of the US Army and the US government.[15]

On August 2, 1814, Washington's *National Intelligencer* published an extract of a letter from a gentleman at Le Roy, dated July 20:

> "On Monday, the 18th instant (*sic*) the village of St Davids was burnt by a detachment of our troops. The place is in sight from the mountain of Lewiston, and when I left there, I could not see but one house remaining, and the burning as not yet finished. I was told that this place was destroyed in consequence of the inhabitants having captured some public teams and murdered an ensign of the Dragoons, St Davids contained mills, and between 20 and 30 dwelling houses."[6]

There is a discrepancy in dates regarding when the burning of St Davids occurred, July 18th or July 19th. It is possible that it took place over both days. At least four buildings survived the incendiary attack: Solomon Quick's Tavern, the gristmill at 137 Four Mile Creek Road, 215 Four Mile Creek Road, and 46 Paxton Lane; 290 Four Mile Creek Road was partly damaged.

The last remaining shell of a burned house from that time was dismantled in 1915 on the creek side of Paxton Lane. It belonged to Mr. William Woodruff and was called the "little red house." It had two bake ovens in the cellar, two large chimneys, and two large fireplaces, one at each end. The rafters and floorboards were put together with wooden pins. The cellar was built of stone and dug into the bank above the creek.

The destruction at York in April 1813, and the burning of homes and other buildings on December 10, 1813, in the Town of Niagara, are well covered in Pierre Berton's *War of 1812*. Here, he describes the feeling of inhabitants in the Niagara region: "In the hearts of the homeless and the soldiers, there is one common emotion: a desire for retaliation. The sense-less burning of the loyalist settlements in the region will send an echo down the corridors of history, it is this act, much more than the accidental firing of the legislature at York, that provokes a succession of incendiary raids that will not end until the city of Washington itself is in flames."[33]

On December 24, 1814, the delegates agreed to the terms of the Treaty of Ghent, and the draft treaty was finally ratified by the British Parliament and the US Congress—on February 16, 1815. In *War of 1812*, Berton reflects: "The war helped set the two countries on different courses. National characteristics were evolving: American ebullience, Canadian reserve. The Americans went wild over minor triumphs, the Canadians remained phleg-matic over major ones."[33,54] American soldiers could become a president (as George Washington did). Liberty was what Americans fought for. "Loyalty meant loyalty to Britain and British values"[33] in Canada; the Crown was still firmly on King George III's head.

LAURA SECORD

The Secord family has always been a big part of the history of St Davids and Laura (Ingersoll) Secord is remembered as the heroine of the day when it comes to the Battle of Beaver Dams. Her story has been told many times (perhaps with embellishment and artistic license) in books, plays, and poetry.

Laura, the daughter of Thomas Ingersoll and Elizabeth Dewey, was the eldest of the family, and only eight years old when her mother died, leaving four little girls. Thomas's second wife died when Laura was just fourteen years old. These tragedies at such an early age were just the beginning of many in a long life of challenging situations.

In 1795, at the age of nineteen, Laura helped her father migrate to Canada with his third wife, Sarah (Sally) Bachus, (née Whiting), and their growing family. Not long after arriving and living in Queenston, Laura met and married James Secord, the younger brother of Major David Secord. Their first home was in St Davids. Her first three children were born there. They later moved to Queenston and were living there when the War of 1812 began.[60]

James, a sergeant of 1st Lincoln Militia in Captain Isaac Swayze's unit of Provincial Royal Artillery Drivers, the Car Brigade,[82] used farm horses to move field guns. He was wounded at the battle of Queenston Heights and carried home to be nursed by Laura. Once there, they discovered their home had been ransacked by invading American soldiers. As winter started to close in, they moved back to St Davids to stay with family until the spring of 1813, when they returned home for James to continue his recovery.

In that same season, the Americans planned another invasion of the Niagara area. On May 27, 1813, they captured Fort George and occupied Niagara for the next several months.

According to legend, American soldiers were stationed in Queenston and two of their officers were billeted at the Secord house. There are different accounts of how Laura overheard a conversation, on June 21, about a plan to attack the British supply depot at DeCew (DeCou) House near Beaver Dams (now Thorold). One such account is documented in Ruth McKenzie's book, *Laura Secord: The Legend and the Lady.*[28] One evening, either Laura or James overheard some Americans talking about an expedition that was about to get underway against the unit commanded by Lieutenant James FitzGibbon of the 49th Regiment. Laura and James immediately realized that FitzGibbon must be warned; however, James was still recuperating from his injuries and could not walk very far. Laura would have to make the journey herself.

Early in the morning of June 22, 1813, she managed to evade the American sentries and set out for St Davids to see her half-brother Charles Ingersoll, who might be able to help. But he was sick in bed with fever and was being looked after by Hannah Secord (Stephen Secord's widow). Charles was engaged to be married to Hannah's eldest daughter, twenty-year-old Elizabeth. Major David Secord was away with the militia and could not help, so Elizabeth offered to go with Laura. To avoid meeting American soldiers, the women decided to take a longer route to DeCew House, via the intersection known as Shipman's Corners, (now St Catherines). Elizabeth became very tired during the journey, and by the time they reached Shipman's Corners, she was slowing her aunt down. The Secord family had friends at Shipman's Corners and Laura left her niece with them.[60]

Laura continued her journey, following the general direction of Twelve Mile Creek. She stumbled through woods and across fields for many hours until she came across a group of First Nations encamped in John DeCew's field. Upon seeing her, they all rose and yelled at her, making her tremble. Overcoming her fear, she managed to convey her important message to one of the chiefs, who took her to DeCew house, which was being used as FitzGibbon's detachment headquarters. The information that she gave to FitzGibbon may have had some importance. On the morning of June 24, the

Americans planned an attack on Beaver Dams but stumbled into an ambush set up by militia captain Dominique Ducharme of the Indian Department.[62] In the ensuing battle, the American force was pinned down by Indigenous allies including those from the Seven Nations of Lower Canada (mostly Iroquoian people),[61] and more than 500 Americans were forced to surrender to FitzGibbon and his men. However, there was no real recognition of Laura's role in the victory at that time.

Even though FitzGibbon acknowledged Laura's part in the victory, her heroic act was forgotten for fifty years until 1860, when Edward, Prince of Wales, came to Canada on a visit. By then, Laura was eighty-five years of age, impoverished, and living in Chippawa, but was still able to convey her story to the prince. After Edward heard it, he did not forget the frail old lady. When he returned to England, he sent a gift of a hundred pounds in gold to her.[60]

Meeting with Lt. FitzGibbon June 1813: Lorne K. Smith
Courtesy: Library and Archives Canada

Eight years later, in 1868, Laura, the female heroine of the veterans of the War of 1812, died at age ninety-three in her home in Chippawa. Her heroism has since been recognized and continues to be remembered. The home in Queenston where Laura and James lived during their young, tumultuous lives has been restored and is open to visitors during the summer months.

Francis Goring

Some of the original settlers who came to the Niagara area in the late 1700s have direct descendants who live in St Davids. Dennis Goring is one of them. A retired teacher and a seventh-generation Goring, he was brought up on the Goring farm a few kilometres west of the village, at Queenston and Townline roads. Dennis moved from the farm in 1985, and lives with his family on Paxton Lane; his ancestry farm was sold for land development in the early 1990s.[7]

Francis Goring (1755-1842), who was born in London, England, was a remarkable young man. At age twenty-one in 1776, he boarded the transport ship *Speke* and sailed to Montreal to meet his employer, Deputy Quartermaster General Gabriel Christie. In August he was sent to Fort Niagara to work as a clerk to Thomas Robison and later as a clerk for George Forsyth and Edward Pollard, who were both involved in the fur trade. His business as a clerk included filling and dispatching supplies for the Butler's Rangers. Between 1780 and 1781, Francis was a partner in the trading firm of Bennet, Goring and Street.[87]

His father, Abraham Goring, was a bookseller who likely immersed young Francis in literature. When Francis arrived at Niagara in August 1776, he was recognized as a literate, intelligent, and well-educated person. Much of what is known about him comes from his letters, account entries, and correspondence. A diary entry describes how he felt about arriving at Fort Niagara:

"There are no pleasures or prospects to direct the mind, being confined to woods on one side and the water on the other. Our whole place consists of a fort, and four houses, and above five hundred men, therefore I leave you to judge how agreeable it must be to one who has [been] accustomed to much pleasure."

Another entry: "This place . . . is out of the world; in the woods and frequented by nothing but Indians. . . . my salary is but small but have now about 50 guineas per annum and flatter myself there is not a clerk in these parts that have so much." He added a comment to this: "having found board and washing."[87]

About 1781, Francis married Lucy Secord (1763-1801), the seventh child of Peter Secord. In 1784, they obtained a land grant from the Crown and began farming on Lots 178, 179, and 180.[25] Francis and Lucy raised a family of ten children. Unfortunately, Lucy died during the winter of 1801, and Francis never remarried.

During his life, Francis kept a diary and recorded trade transactions, crops he planted and harvested, the animals he butchered and sold, lists of his students, and visits of dignitaries. He only mentions the birth of two of his children: a son on August 10, 1792, and a daughter on May 26, 1794.

For many years, Francis was a land agent and secretary to Robert Hamilton, the county land agent for the District of Nassau. He was also a notable teacher. His diary entries[87] reflect the following:

> 1790— "Kept no school from Nov 23,"
> 1791—January 23, "gave it up on account [their] not providing a stove, keeping me out of employ,"
> 1791—February 7, "moved from the schoolhouse at Three Mile Creek,"
> 1791—February 10, "moved to my farm,"
> 1791—February 25, "raised a schoolhouse at Six Mile Creek."

He listed his students' names, including neighbours and children. He also mentions that he schooled Robert Hamilton's children. There were no textbooks available in those days, so he wrote his own, creating texts on such subjects as geometry, astronomy, and mathematics using a quill pen, and ink made by Indigenous people living in the area.[73] In 1792, Francis' name was the first on a petition to Governor Simcoe requesting a road to be built connecting Queenston to St Davids, now York Road.

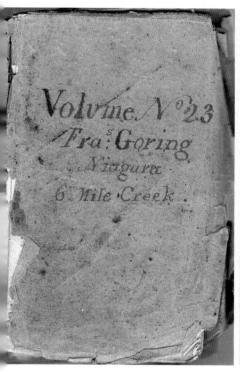

Francis Goring's Journal Vol. 23
Courtesy: Dennis Goring

Francis Goring's calculation of equal division
of land with common pond.
Courtesy: Dennis Goring

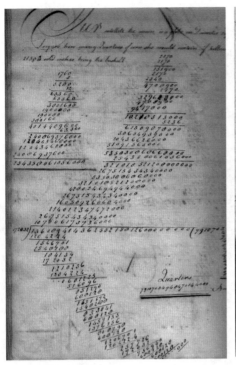

How many quarters of corn will fill the moon?

Courtesy: Dennis Goring

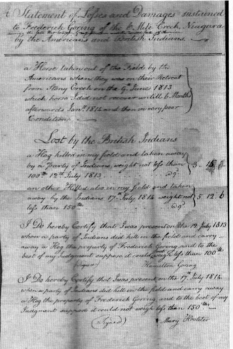

Frederick Goring (son of Francis):

Claim for Losses 1813-14

Courtesy: Dennis Goring

Francis wrote many interesting stories and poetry. One such thoughtful piece is worth a mention:

Childhood

"Childhood is like a mirror, catching and reflecting images from all around it. Remember that an injurious or profane thought uttered by a parent line (*sic*) may operate on a young heart like staining it with rust, which no after scouring can efface."[87]

Francis taught school for many years and lived to be eighty-seven. His life ended in 1842. He is buried in Homer Cemetery, but with the ravages of time, no grave marker can be identified.

In his will, signed August 26, 1833, Francis left land and money to his children. He also left a silver punch ladle to his friend Richard Woodruff of St Davids. He writes: "Think when this you use and see, you will, I hope, remember me."[7]

Francis's descendants have been active through the generations. Many served in the armed forces and some maintained a tradition of public service: A sixth generation born on the Goring farm was Frederick Stewart Goring (1923-1989), a bomber pilot during WWII, a politician, and the first Lord Mayor (1970-1973) of the new municipality of the Town of Niagara-on-the-Lake. He was also warden for Lincoln County.

St Davids School

The first school in the St Davids vicinity, Six Mile School, was a one-room structure built in 1791[87] by Francis Goring on his farm at Six Mile Creek. It was made of logs, and later was replaced by a thirty-foot, square-framed cottage building. Parents paid money directly to him for his services. For example, his neighbour Christian Warner paid him seven pounds sterling for schooling his children from 1796 to 1797.[2,87]

In 1814, most buildings in St Davids were destroyed by American troops. In 1816, Major David Secord donated land for a school to be built where the United Church and cemetery are today. It remained in use until 1871, when David Jackson Lowrey donated a bell and land for a new school to be built on the current location on York Road. In 1921, Charlton Goring's wife, Viola Stuart, was a teacher in the school.

In 1834, author Emma Currie remembered her school days in St Davids and described what it was like to be a student in the nineteenth century:

> "My brother and I went to the public school, which was on part of the land given by Major David Secord. . . . The teacher at that time was Mr. Dennis Hanlan. . . . At that time, the scholars took their turn to keep the school room tidy. The boys brought in the wood for the stove and went for the water to drink. The girls swept and dusted the class-room. There were no steel pens in those days; the teacher had to prepare the quill pens. Those that could afford to

buy one purchased it in the store and were called 'clarified quills.' Some sought in the creek, where many geese were to be seen, for wing feathers from the many geese to be made into quill pens. A large stove stood in the centre of the schoolroom and wood was piled on the floor under the stove. The desks were located at the upper end—one long, one short on the side, and the small children sat in the lower benches, without a back, in front of the desks, of which were only six in the room. The windows were un-curtained, a bench with the pail of water and a tin cup from which all drank stood at the entrance of the school room."[59]

Emma Currie continued to be taught in the school until she was nine or ten years old.

In 1914, at the start of WWI, two rooms were added for Grade 7 and 8 students. Then in 1953, the old one-room classroom was removed and replaced with two new ones, plus a playroom; a third addition was completed in 1960.

In the fall of 1990, the Lincoln County Board decided to add a gymnasium, and construction began in September 1991. Then in 1994, a new library/computer room, offices, and entrance hall were built.[9]

Today in the twenty-first century, St Davids School is vibrant, and its student population is growing. The school has fourteen teachers, from junior and senior kindergarten and grades 1 through 8. It continues to teach to high academic literacy standards and parental participation in the school is encouraged. If Francis Goring could visit St Davids School today and see the outcome of his love for teaching, it is guaranteed that he would feel proud of how far education has come over the last 200 plus years.

1910 view of St Davids schoolhouse on York Road looking west.
Courtesy: Niagara Falls Public Library

1918 St Davids schoolchildren
Courtesy: Gail Woodruff

St Davids schoolchildren c.1920

Courtesy: Gail Woodruff

St Davids School 2017

Photograph courtesy: G.F. Walker

School bell commemorative plaque
Photograph courtesy: G.F. Walker

9

Village Development

In the 1780s, most refugees arriving on the west bank of the Niagara River were destitute but determined to build a new life, despite the enormous task of clearing land in the undisturbed wilderness.

For cabin construction and business development it was necessary to fell trees; fortunately, the refugees had many essential skills and, when they surveyed land for building mills, they took note of the power of the crystal-clear water of Four Mile Creek. The creek was alive with many species of fish, and all around there was an abundance of rabbits, quail, wild ducks, and geese.[1,38]

Between 1782 and 1812, the settlers lived up to all expectations. They cleared the land, built homes, laid down crops, and raised farm animals. St Davids became a flourishing community. They built four gristmills; a sawmill; a distillery; a tannery; and a shoe, soap, candle, and barrel factory. Four Mile Creek supplied water power for these businesses. The village had two churches, a school, and approximately forty homes. It had a daily mail delivery service from Queenston.

When the Americans declared war in June 1812, the lives of the settlers here changed. They were under a constant threat of invasion, and then their homes were destroyed in 1814. It was the leadership of David Secord and Richard Woodruff that enabled their collective spirit to rise from the ashes. The settlers rebuilt their lives and community, and their homes and businesses were eventually replaced. The farms started to produce meat, vegetables, fruit, and eggs, and food became plentiful again.

In 1815, one of the first businesses to be built was the Richard Woodruff general store on the south corner of York Road and Four Mile Creek. Richard operated it until his death in 1872, when George Woodruff became the

owner. Between 1893 and 1896, Edwin David Lowrey owned it. Then his brother Matthew took it over. He added two wings to the building and operated it until 1910. Edwin David then took the store back and part of it became a post office; he ran the store until 1918, when Archie Woodruff bought it, and operated it until the late 1920s. Ida May Woodruff was post mistress prior to the property being demolished in 1961, when road widening occurred along York Road.[29]

Woodruff general store built in 1815.
Its ownership later changed between the
Woodruff and Lowrey families.
Courtesy: Niagara Historical Society & Museum

Woodruff store extended c.1918
Courtesy: Niagara Historical Society & Museum

In the spring of 1816, Richard Cockrell, the founding editor of *The Spectator*, started printing editions on the premises of 1367 York Road.[55] This was the first newspaper in the St Davids area, and its columns were filled with names of dead and wounded militiamen, and of the widows and children of those who died. It also reported on relief pensions and grants awarded to war victims. The paper was especially useful for advertising dry goods and groceries, and for informing folks of events.[35]

The Spectator; the first newspaper in the area.
Vol. 1, No. 8., dated Friday March 22, 1816

In 1816, *The Spectator* printed two notices concerning Henry Augustus Woodruff and Timothy Street. The issue, dated March 22, informed the public of the partnership of Woodruff and Street Saddlery and Harnessing business in the village of St Davids. Unfortunately, the partnership was short-lived, and in the May 3 issue the public were notified of the dissolution of the business, and it was announced that "Street and Woodruff, saddlers" would be carried on by Timothy Street.[29]

In February 1817, the paper became known as the *Niagara Spectator*, and in August, the office was moved to Niagara, where Amos McKenney became its publisher, followed by Bartemas Ferguson, who was later prosecuted and imprisoned for his political opinions. Despite this, the paper continued to be printed for many years.

In 1818, the first steam gristmill in Ontario was built behind 215 Four Mile Creek. It was later used as a fruit evaporator by the Lowrey brothers, and was eventually demolished.

Between 1800 and 1820, a Black community owned small farms at the south end of Tanbark Road, in the current area of Highway 405. These farms were later bought out and became the Hanniwell farm. One family—the Grahams—refused to sell, and their descendants by the name of Hedgeman were the last residents of this group in St Davids.[35]

In 1836, John Sleeman, originally from Cornwall, England, built the Stamford Spring Brewery and Distillery on the west side of Four Mile Creek.[19] In 1847, I. A. Hatt bought the brewery and made it such a success that even the young boys tried out the beer on one occasion. "It was a Saturday morning in the late 1840s, and most of the older boys had arrived at school ahead of the new schoolmaster. They ordered the girls home, and demanded beer money from the schoolmaster before they would let him in. He foolishly gave in and the boys used the money to buy beer. By midmorning, most were intoxicated. But as one observer put it, good came out of evil, as the young boys suffered so much from the effects of the beer that they grew up to be sober men."[1]

In the 1850s, James Oswald owned the brewery. He sold it to William Henry in the early 1860s. Henry enlarged it, installed a fountain and fish pond out front, and made it the best-known business in the St Davids area. The brewery operated until after WWI, when Mrs. E. Homer Dixon bought it and made it profitable by bottling spring water there from Four Mile Creek. The water was distributed through the Spring Water Bottling Works in Niagara Falls and sold to upscale grocery stores in Niagara Falls, New York. The bottling plant expanded its business by shipping spring water all over southern Ontario. Later, interest in spring water declined, and the facility was abandoned. It fell into ruin, ending over ninety years of commercial enterprise. After the turn of the century, the building was used as a recreation and dance hall called the Ravine Inn. It eventually burned down.[19,67]

St Davids Spring Mill Distillery and Brewery c.1862
Courtesy: Niagara Falls Public Library

The area that is called the Queenston Quarry today was carved from land partly owned by the Secord Family.[25] It stretches along the top of the Niagara Escarpment from the east side of St Davids several kilometres towards Queenston Heights. The area just east of St Davids became notable for the best building stone, and by the beginning of the 1830s the St Davids quarries were described as having an inexhaustible supply of a unique stone called Lockport Dolomite. The quarry was "high-graded," i.e. that is mined selectively for the best stone—in this case, the Gasport layer.[88] This special blue dolomite was sought after for some of Canada's most notable stone buildings. Landmarks such as the Canadian parliament buildings, Queen's Park, Toronto's Union Station, the courthouse in Niagara-on-the-Lake, and Brock's Monument. It was also shipped as far away as London, England. The name "Queenston quarries" first appeared in 1936 and was used when referring to the numerous quarries under varied ownership on the Escarpment above St Davids.[46]

In 1838, John Brown, a Scottish-stonecutter and masonry contractor, came to Canada from the US and began working at the quarry. By 1842 he consolidated the 150-acre quarry lands and, in 1848, sold them to Samuel H. Smith. In 1861, Smith sold the lands to William Hendershot. The Hendershot company was one of ten, which together provided employment to as many as 600 workers. In 1876, William Hendershot was the major operator.[88]

Quarry operations
Courtesy: Niagara Historical Society & Museum

The quarry continued to be productive through the years and, between 1905 and 1924, the Lowrey family operated it and its associated stone crushing operation. During that time, the stone crusher was twice rebuilt, and hand-operated saws were replaced by power-driven ones. From 1923 to 1947, Paul Woodruff was the works manager. He was followed in this role by his son Richard, who was general manager between 1974 and 2006.

The site is currently undergoing a major redevelopment and the prized Queenston limestone on the 245-acre quarry continues to be extracted for monuments and heritage restoration. In the coming years, it will be used on the homes and buildings of a residential community that will feature a host of agricultural and open-space recreational areas. The master plan includes walking trails connecting to the Bruce Trail, organic gardens, sculpture gardens, a conservatory, perennial gardens, an amphitheatre, a beach, pools, a spa, an equestrian centre, a golf academy, a vineyard, subterranean in-rock wine cellars that will be cut into the vertical rock faces, a farm-to-table restaurant, a café, a general store, and an art gallery. The developer and project co-owner is local resident and lawyer, Frank Racioppo.[46]

Let us go back to the post-war recovery. By 1850, the population of St Davids had grown. Fruit growing had been introduced to the region, and this enterprise had gradually replaced mixed farming as the main industry. Fruits such as peaches, plums, sour cherries, and apricots were grown here. David Jackson Lowrey is credited with bringing the first commercial vineyard to the district in or around 1869. Today, David Jackson's great-grandchildren are still operating the vineyards.

In 1851, a tannery was still operating (William Kirby, of literary fame, worked there as a tanner in 1839).[26] The village post office was operated by the Lowrey family. There was an implement business known for its excellent ploughs and a village blacksmith.

In the mid-1860s, the population numbered about 300, and the village had a hotel, a school with forty pupils, and a church for all denominations.[1,65] The roads were not good, and transportation was not easy, so local trades supported village needs. There was a harness maker, Jim Brown was the village's rough carpenter, and if anyone wanted a cabinet to be made, they asked Jimmy Jones. Blacksmiths (Jim McSherry, Jim Robinson, and Jim Smith) kept horses shoed and made implements to work the ground. C. A. Simpson made shoes and repaired them when required.[1]

CA Simpson Shoemaker and Harness Repair
Courtesy: Niagara Falls Public Library

In 1885, Isaac Usher and son leased a portion of the Queenston Quarry from William Hendershot and opened a cement operation above York Road, close to St Davids. The Ushers mined a natural layer of rock cement, fired it in limestone kilns, ground it into powder, and barreled the finished product. It was then loaded onto carriages on a spur line of the Michigan Central

Railway. Two surviving houses in the village were made of Usher cement
(167 and 234 Creek Road). The cement works ceased operation in 1905
amidst competition from the quicker-setting Portland Cement product.[1,53]

Harold Usher with a shipment of Blue Dolomite
Courtesy: Niagara Historical Society & Museum

Stone crushers at the Cement Works
c. 1927
Courtesy: Niagara Falls
Public Library

Quarry workers
Courtesy: Richard Woodruff

In 1886, the Silver Lake Canning Company was located on the east side of
Creek Road near where Highway 405 crosses over it. It was built by Charles
and George Black, and was probably the first St Davids canning factory. Its
principal products were fruits and tomato ketchup. The factory operated for
thirty-five years until 1921. In 1923, Dominion Canning Ltd., bought it, but
never operated it.[35] Dominion Canning Ltd., eventually became part of the
Canadian Canners Ltd.

In 1893, a long-distance telephone line was started from Niagara Falls to St Davids. In 1894, Edwin David Lowrey managed the central telephone office in the village. Only two customers were listed in the directory: fruit grower E. D. Lowrey and Edwin Terrill, from the local gravel works. Between 1907 and 1908, thirteen customers were listed. It was the last time St Davids was listed as a separate exchange. In the fall of 1908, telephone lines were connected with the Niagara Falls exchange.[67]

In 1897, Frank and Harry Lowrey purchased the gristmill near the old Kraft Canning Factory on Creek Road and converted it into a factory for canning fruits and vegetables, also jams and jellies. Between 1903 and 1904, it became part of Canadian Canners Ltd. It operated until 1923, when it burned down; it was rebuilt in 1924.[35,67]

Lowrey Canning Factory c.1900
Courtesy: Niagara Falls Public Library

At the turn of the century, St Davids was still a bustling community. There were two general stores, four gristmills, three blacksmiths, a barrel factory, and one hotel.

In 1904, the Usher Canning Factory was one of three in the area. It was located at the base of the escarpment, south of the intersection at Concession 2 and York Road, next to Ushers Cement Works. Usher built the factory in 1904, and operated it until 1915. Dominion Canners Ltd. bought the factory in 1919, and used it for storage until 1932.[35]

The Doyle Hotel operated where the Avondale Convenience Store is today. It was a large brick building with a livery stable. In 1910, the hotel and stable caught fire and flames could be seen for miles.

In 1918, Canadian Canners Ltd., required more spring water for its operations, so started to install a water line from the flowing springs up near the ravine hill. The water line was completed in 1919, and residents of St Davids, for the first time, had running water in their homes. This meant no more carrying water, wash-tub baths, or outdoor toilets.[35,67]

In 1923, Howard Slingerland moved to St Davids and bought William (Scotty) Burnett's gristmill, which was in the gully behind the current Bank building on Four Mile Creek. The original mill may have been the sawmill built for Peter and James Secord in 1783. It was burned down in 1814, and later rebuilt by David Secord.[35] The water-powered mill was fed from a millpond via an aqueduct located further up the gully along the west side. When the aqueduct deteriorated, Howard operated the mill with an electric motor. In the 1940s, electricity costs increased, so he changed the power source to gasoline. He purchased a Ford V8 engine, which he mounted and fitted so that the exhaust would exit the building via the roof.

Local farmers brought oats and wheat to be ground. The mill also shelled and ground corn until 1929, when it closed and was demolished.[32]

Slingerland Mill behind the old Bank building
Courtesy: Niagara Falls Public Library

Don Slingerland, son of Howard, a long-time resident of St Davids, recalls that around 1929, his father built a grocery store adjacent to the mill, which was operated by the family until the 1970s. At one point, it was split into two businesses to include a pharmacy. His father managed the grocery store and rented space to Mr. Pew for the pharmacy. The pharmacy also had an ice cream parlour; ice cream was served in paper cones in V-shaped silver metal dishes. Mr. Pew operated the pharmacy until he died in the 1930s. In 1945, the dividing wall between the two stores was removed. Howard's son Carl began helping with the store, and eventually took it over in the 1950s. When Carl retired, it was leased to a Mr. Sante, followed by a Mr. Paul Maatz.[32]

In 1924, a bus route operated from St Davids to Niagara Falls and St Catharines. It also took children to Niagara Falls High School; before this, the children and people without cars had to walk to the St Davids station, a mile from the four stop signs in the village.[67]

The building known as the "fruit barn" on Four Mile Creek Road, (near Creekside Drive) was built by Darcy Cropp on farm land where he grew fruits. The farm was north of Highway 405, as it passes over Four Mile Creek Road, and continued down to Johanna Drive in the village. Darcy also had a canning factory in Niagara Falls.

The Fedorkow family, originally from the Ukraine, came to Canada around 1912, returned to the Ukraine after WWI, and then returned in the early 1920s. They lived first in Montreal, then moved to the province of Manitoba. From there, with their six children, they moved to Ontario. After living in Hamilton, they moved to Niagara and bought a farm east of St Davids. In 1940, they purchased the Darcy Cropp fruit farm, which they called "J. Fedorkow and Sons." They grew strawberries, raspberries, both sweet and sour cherries, peaches, plums, and pears, which they shipped to local markets and canneries and sold to wholesalers. In those days the tourist steamship *Cayuga* made regular sailings between Queenston and Toronto and Fedorkow fruits were loaded on the Queenston dock to be shipped to wholesalers in Toronto where the fresh-picked fruit was sold to Torontonians.

During WWII, there was a shortage of help to harvest fruit crops and the Ontario provincial government set up a program for high school and university students to be employed during the season to help with picking fruits. These young girls, called "Farmerettes," were housed in a building behind the fruit barn and at a hotel in Queenston. Many local Niagara farmers took advantage of the Farmerette program throughout the war years.

Many years later, the Fedorkow farm was divided between William and his brother Walter. The children of Walter inherited land when their father died, and parts of the farm have been sold over the years. Much of the land has now been used for new housing developments.

Walter's son John continues the tradition of fruit farming, including a vineyard on Line 8 Road, just north of St Davids.[85]

In 1960, St Davids had 520 residents and boasted four gas stations: at the current Creekside Senior Estates, Avondale store, the corner where the new dental office is, and Gales Gas Station on York Road.

Before 1963, Four Mile Creek Road going south went through a tunnel, which traffic and pedestrians used to reach Stamford and Niagara Falls. The tunnel, built in 1853, went under the great Western Railway and was sealed up when Highway 405 was completed in 1963.[5]

In 1965, St Davids underwent a drastic change. Many stately old trees lining the main thoroughfare(s) were cut down in a highway-widening project. The Lowrey general store on the corner of the four stop signs was levelled to make the intersection safer. The old tannery ruins and the last of the old mills were demolished when the road was elevated. At that time, St Davids lost many of its historic landmarks.[5] From then onward, St Davids continued as a small community known for its fruit orchards and expanding vineyards. Small businesses appeared and disappeared. During the summer, there was always a fruit and vegetable market and families here enjoyed a quiet, rural lifestyle.

When the millennium arrived, St Davids started to expand with the growth of housing developments, and young people and baby boomers began to discover the village. In 2017, businesses in the village included a chocolate factory, a winery and restaurant, a Mediterranean restaurant, a dental office, a corner store, a rehabilitation gym, a financial services office, a real estate office, various bed and breakfasts, a gas station, a veterinary clinic, a post office, and a home décor store.

In 2017, St Davids population was approaching 2,000, and it is projected to grow to 4,200 by 2030.

Jerman's Gas Station and Refreshment Stand
Courtesy: Niagara Falls Public Library

Shamrock Inn Tourist Home c.1930
Courtesy: Niagara Falls Public Library

Old Oak Inn and Toutist Camp, Highway No. 8, St Davids Ontario, Canada

Courtesy: Niagara Falls Public Library

Four Mile Creek Road looking south c.1918
Courtesy: Niagara Falls Public Library

Highway 8 (York Road) looking east early 1900s
Courtesy: Niagara Falls Public Library

Four Mile Creek Road looking north c. 1920
Courtesy: Niagara Historical Society & Museum

John Fedorkow and Sons Fruit Barn and Packing Shed 1965 & 2018. The barn was moved from its 1965 location to the west end of the adjacent packing shed.
1965 photograph courtesy: John Fedorkow;
2018 photograph courtesy: G.F. Walker

10

LOWREY FAMILY

David Jackson Lowrey (1824-1901), son of Matthew Lowrey and Hannah Kelly, married Elizabeth Catherine Teeter (1826-1912) in 1849. They would go on to have ten children (six sons and four daughters). Catherine was a granddaughter of U.E. George Caughill. More information on the descendants of David Jackson can be found in Chapter 19.

In 1867, David Jackson Lowrey bought the Upper family farm in St Davids and started planting vegetables and fruit trees in 1868. In 1869, he started farming commer-

Courtesy: Niagara-on-the-Lake Public Library

cial grape vines; since then, his descendants have continued to grow many kinds of grapes.[36] Three of his sons became prominent businessmen in St Davids and its vicinity.

Matthew Charles Lowrey, first son of David Jackson Lowrey, was born at Vanessa, Ontario, in 1855. He moved to St Davids with his parents at age twenty-five, and started work in the milling business. He married Helen Emily Wallace and had five children; later in life, he married Mary McBride.

Matthew Charles and Helen Emily Lowrey
Courtesy: Niagara-on-the-Lake Public Library

Matthew Charles (right) outside his store
Courtesy: Niagara-on-the-Lake Public Library

By 1891, Matthew Charles had become a well-known Niagara business-man. He first started a canning factory at Niagara-on-the-Lake, which he later sold. He then opened the Lowrey Canning Factory in St Davids. He also owned general stores, including ones in Niagara Falls, St Davids, and

Queenston. He was postmaster at Queenston for thirteen years, and president of the Queenston Quarries in the late 1800s. He was also Deputy Reeve in Niagara Township. He died at Queenston in 1931.

Edwin David Lowrey,[36] second son of David Jackson Lowrey, was born in Windham, Ontario, in 1859. In adult life, he became interested in the affairs of the village and was involved with a construction company in partnership with Ed. Ferris, Fred Goring, and a Mr. Sutherland. He owned a controlling interest in the Queenston Quarry Company, which he later sold to his brother Matthew Charles in 1910.

In 1893, he purchased the Richard Woodruff (King Dick) store. In 1896, his brother Matthew Charles took the business over and ran it until 1910. He then took the store back and operated it until 1918, when Archie Woodruff bought it. He retired to his 150-acre farm and started developing and improving various varieties of fruit. He died in 1950 at age ninety-one.

In 2018, the Lowrey family are still business minded people and own vineyards and a restaurant.

Edwin David Lowrey
Courtesy: Niagara-on-the-Lake
Public Library

11

Bank Robberies

One would not expect a small village like St Davids to be the scene of bank robberies. But perhaps because it was and still is a quiet place to live, robbers considered the Imperial Bank an easy target on four separate occasions. Only one of them was successful. There were long intervals between attempts, but violence and shooting were part of each one.

In a well-planned attempt involving eight men in 1907, robbers entered the village in the early hours of the morning in horse-drawn vehicles and blocked the road at the Old Mill Inn on Four Mile Creek and at the Fudge Stand on York Road. While two men guarded each intersection and watched the horses, other gang members tried to remove the door of the safe with nitroglycerine. By coincidence, it happened that the bank teller was returning to the bank from Niagara Falls after having had a good night out. When stopped by the picket at the Old Mill, he was considered a harmless, good-natured drunk, and they let him pass. Approaching the bank, he was somewhat sobered up by the blast of the first explosion, which removed the outer door of the safe. He ran to the back of the building and began hurling stones through the rear windows. The robbers responded by discharging their guns. When lights came on in nearby homes, they panicked and fled with their horse and buggies. They did not realize that only a thin wooden door lay between them and $5,000. When in a more-sober condition, the teller was rewarded by the bank.

A second robbery, in 1923, was attempted single-handedly before dawn by a man who broke into the living quarters of bank manager Mr. Russell

Rogers. A kitten jumping on Mr. Rogers's bed woke him up. Remembering that he had locked the kitten outside, he immediately suspected that someone had broken into the building. Leaving his bedroom, he encountered a bullet that grazed his forehead. He lunged at the robber to prevent a second shot being fired. The two men then wrestled their way to the balcony at the rear of the building. The more powerful robber almost hurled Rogers from the balcony when the voice of Mrs. Archie Woodruff threatened to fire her shotgun from a window, with Mr. Rogers's permission! Knowing the spreading qualities of shot from such a gun, he pleaded with her to stop because she could hurt both men. At that moment, a shot rang out and the robber collapsed and later died from a bullet discharged from Mr. Rogers's own revolver fired through a screen door by Mrs. Rogers, who had never handled a gun before!

Just before 3 p.m. on August 16, 1951, when the bank was due to close, two men successfully robbed it of $6,000. The front-page headline of the *Evening Review* read: "Brave Woman Teller Saves $27,000, St Davids Holdup." The teller, Ann Neufeld, managed to sound the alarm while two bandits were scooping notes into a bag at her wicket. Another teller, eighteen-year old Robert Izett, shot at the robbers three times before they escaped in a stolen car. The two suspects—one from Buffalo and one from Toronto—were apprehended a few weeks later.

Three young bandits tried to rob the bank on September 12, 1951. In this case, a teller and the bank manager foiled the attempt. The teller activated the warning siren, and the manager wounded two of the bandits. Carl Slingerland, who managed a nearby grocery store, fired shots into the tires of the getaway car stolen from lawyer Judy LaMarsh. A customer in the bank fired shots at the fleeing bandits using the manager's revolver. Two wounded suspects were captured later in the day and a third was captured a few hours after.[10,13,67]

12

VILLAGE STORIES

Over the last several generations, for whatever reason, Devil's Night, or Cabbage Night (the eve before Halloween), has been celebrated with great gusto in the village, and a considerable number of notorious pranks have been carried out. When people in St Davids get together over a glass of wine, stories of these times gone by invariably fill the air, and many took place on that infamous night. Here—with names withheld to protect innocent descendants—are some of the more memorable ones. They have been either passed down as folklore or personally witnessed.

HOWIE LOWREY, 2017:

Circa 1930s, farm equipment (wagons, manure spreaders, buggies, mowers, etc.) were collected from surrounding farms during the night before Halloween and placed on the large veranda of the Woodruff-Lowrey general store. The fun part was watching everyone the next day arriving and deciding which equipment belonged to which farmer.

Each year the challenge had been to remove Mrs. Paxton's cow Daisy from her barn and tie her up in the centre of the village. One year, Mrs. Paxton decided she would make sure Daisy was secure, and so went to great lengths locking and barricading all entrances to her barn. The pranksters were not deterred. They removed several boards from the back of the barn and triumphantly led Daisy away once again. The next morning, the frustrated Mrs. Paxton again had to find her cow! What is unclear is if the barn needed repair.

One Devils' Night in the 1960s, Major Bruce Woodruff's white horse was painted pink. Everyone knew who the culprits were because they had painted their old Model A car the same colour several days before. Unfortunately, the poor horse died shortly after, supposedly from licking the lead-based paint from his body. It is unknown if the perpetrators were punished.

During construction of Highway 405, some enterprising youths managed to obtain blinking warning lights and construction signs to set up a detour and roadblock at the intersection of Swayze Road, Hanniwell Road, and Highway 8 (now known as Tanbark and York roads). Traffic was directed southward up Henley's Hill (top of Tanbark Road) to a dead end, where unsuspecting vehicles, including a Canada Coach bus, were pelted with tomatoes.[36]

Richard Woodruff, 2017:

The business-minded Woodruff family has a rich history of generosity and kindness. The family has many stories from the past, one of these highlights was the rescue of a small baby from the shore of the Niagara River.

During the 1850s, Richard Hall Woodruff (King Dick) and his son Richard Napoleon were out one day shooting game at the Queenston flats (just south of the present dock) when they heard a commotion down on the river bank. During their investigation, they discovered a newborn baby of African American descent. The story passed down from generation to generation in the Woodruff family is that the mother and father had somehow attempted to reach Canada by the Niagara River (how is unknown). In a last act of love, the baby was either placed or thrown on to the shore in the hope that someone would find him; in doing so, they disappeared and perhaps, due to exhaustion, drowned. The baby was rescued and taken to the Woodruffs' home, Locust Hall, in St Davids, and brought up as a family helper. He was named Bill Graham.

Two generations later, Richard Woodruff's Aunt Nora recalled that Bill lived in a small building where the garage of Locust Hall is today. One cold winter's night, she came out from her bedroom to sit by the fireplace and sat next to Bill, who also had come in from the cold. As they sat together in the warmth, Bill said, "This is no place for a white woman to be sitting next to a Black man, Missy Nora." As time went by, kind, compassionate Doc Woodruff (Richard Napoleon's son) bought Bill a small farm west of Tanbark Road and south of Warner Road. Bill lived there until the late 1920s, when he passed away. Bill wanted a "Black family" funeral, and the only people allowed near the body were Doc and son Paul Woodruff. Paul drove a Democrat farm wagon, complete with a black horse, through St Davids with Bill's body lying inside. Also sitting in the wagon was Aunt Nora playing a small piano. Doc walked behind the wagon playing his cornet. Bill, who perhaps was in his 70s, was laid to rest in an unmarked grave in St Davids Cemetery.[29]

DON SLINGERLAND, 2017:

Don recalls that as a young boy he went fishing with his father below the big "Power House" on River Road, where he kept a sled with a big, framed crank, fishing net, and alarm bell. He also had a little shack where a local vagrant holed up, who would always oblige Don's father by dragging the frame into the water downstream. The current would sweep the fish into the net and, when full, the bell would alarm. Each haul would include salmon, white bass, sturgeon, herring, and lots of pickerel. On one occasion, they caught a sturgeon weighing 145 pounds with a roe worth $65. Some people would come down to the bank to buy fish; the rest was taken to Niagara (now Niagara-on-the-Lake) to Mr. Ball and Mr. Bishop, who ran a fish-processing business. Don is currently eighty-eight years of age.[32]

13

Railways

Construction of the Erie and Ontario Railroad started in 1835 and began its train service between Queenston and Chippawa during 1838-1839. The Queenston terminus ended near Brock's monument because the horses couldn't pull the railcars up the steep grade of the escarpment. The passenger cars had four wheels and were pulled along by a team of horses on tracks, which were made of wooden rails topped with iron strips. One car could hold approximately twenty passengers and any luggage was stored on the roof. The driver had an outside roof-level seat and controlled the speed of the horses at about five-miles per hour. The railroad only operated in the busy summer season when passenger traffic was high. It ran west along the southside of York Road and began a gentle climb up the Niagara Escarpment to the Queenston Quarry area. It then followed a pathway southward along the westside of Concession 2 (Stanley Avenue going towards Niagara Falls). At Portage Road, the horses pulling the car were switched for a fresh team to continue the remainder of the journey. The terrain of the railroad running south towards Chippawa was generally flat and required fewer horses.[83]

In 1854, the horse-drawn cars were replaced by steam engines and the Erie and Ontario Railroad was extended to Niagara (now Niagara-on-the-Lake). It followed the original track until it reached St Davids, where it branched off and followed a route down the escarpment to Concession 2 Road, crossing York Road via a bridge (the remnants of the southern abutment can still be seen). It then went north and east towards Concession 1. The tracks would have crossed the intersection of Line 9 and Concession

1, and then paralleled Concession 1, on the east side all the way north in a straight line to Niagara-on-the-Lake. The St Davids Station was built at the intersection of York Road and Concession 2 Road.[83] The station operated until the Railroad closed in 1959. The building was moved to a different location on York Road, and is now a private residence. The Erie and Ontario Railroad became Erie and Niagara Railroad in 1863, Canadian Southern Railroad in 1869, and the Michigan Central Railroad in 1882.

In 1863, George Patrick "Paddy Miles" joined the Erie and Niagara Railroad. He became a much-loved conductor on the train, which was affectionately known as "The Paddy Miles Express," that ran daily from Fort Erie to Niagara.[84]

In 1871, a military camp was established along the shore of the Niagara River. "The Paddy Miles Express" was used to transport troops, supplies and tourists. Unfortunately, in 1959, the railroad was closed.[84]

In the 1920s, there was a time when a steam locomotive with rubber wheels pulled a carriage through the village of St Davids.[1] It is unknown how long this service was available or who operated it.

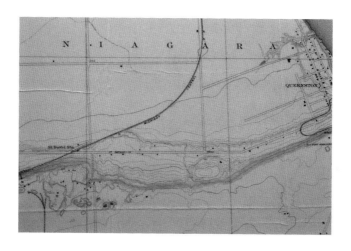

Michigan Central railroad showing St Davids station
Courtesy: Richard Woodruff

St Davids Station looking north (left) and south (right)
Courtesy: Laura Grant (Photographer: John Fryseng)

Railroad bridge over York Road

Courtesy: Richard Woodruff

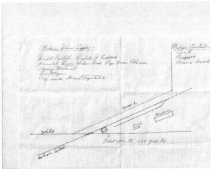

Sketch showing location of St Davids station

Courtesy: Laura Grant

Ravine Hill and tunnel looking north towards St Davids

Courtesy: Niagara Falls Public Library

14

FIREFIGHTERS

Frank Pearson, the current fire chief of the Niagara Firefighters Station No. 2 in St Davids provided access to the minutes journal that was kept from the time the fire department was started for Niagara Township on February 21, 1941. Out of respect for the scribes who recorded the monthly minutes for the organization, their text has only been adjusted where necessary to clarify its meaning.

A first meeting was organized in the Murdoch Hall in St Davids. Fifty people from all parts of the township gathered, including members from the Stamford Fire Department.

> "The first officers and committee members were elected, and Geo Black became the first fire chief. Some of the first decisions included the following: the initial membership fee would be $1.00 for the first year, and 50 cents for every year following. It was agreed that meetings would be held monthly, and minutes were to be recorded in a ledger by hand. The formation of an entertainment committee was agreed upon, along with the decision that proceeds from

each dance would be given to charity. At the end of each meeting, 'God Save the King' was always sung."

The next meeting was held on February 28, 1941: A committee was appointed to draw up departmental bylaws.

> "It was agreed that they would purchase such equipment as three extinguishers, twelve five-gallon water pump extinguishers with ten-foot hoses, and thirty-six water buckets. All would be made available to the villages of St Davids, Queenston, and Virgil."

March 14, 1941: "A report was given to the department regarding equipment for fire prevention in schools. It was discovered that the St Davids School equipment had not been inspected since 1930."

April 3, 1941: "The entertainment committee reported that a card party and dance would be held in the Memorial Hall in Queenston on April 9; it was agreed all proceeds were to go to the Evening Telegram War Victims Fund."

May 9, 1941: "Two fires were reported, one on April 25 and another on April 26. A car of manure had caught fire at Bright's Farms, as (*sic*) had a roof at Peter Wall's farm."

On August 5, 1941: "A barn on Victor Mori's property was burned to the ground, however the garage and chicken coop on the property were saved."

August 8, 1941: "Instruction was given on how to deal with a fire bomb and chimney fires."

October 10, 1941: "A plane had been reported as (*sic*) having crashed and burst into flames near Mrs. Field's Farm. Within seven minutes, the fire brigade reached the site with two four-gallon Fomite extinguishers and put out the blaze. The pilot's body was successfully prevented from being cremated."

January 9, 1942: "A plane made a forced landing on Larkin Farm. Assistant Chief Sheppard quickly went to assist the pilot and found him uninjured; he stayed with him until the Air Force arrived."

January 23, 1942: "St Davids Presbyterian Church caught fire. Members of the fire brigade immediately arrived at the scene. Villagers helped the men with the pumps and organized a line to pass buckets of water, this kept up a continuous flow of water from the creek to the church. This stopped the fire from spreading until the Stamford firemen arrived. They entered the building wearing gas masks and were able to put the fire out."

An article in an old newspaper reports: "Twenty-five women and men formed a human bucket-bridge (*sic*) from a small creek running through the village of St Davids. A fire had broken out in the basement, which was caused by spontaneous combustion of an old quilt. Five years previously, it had been stuffed into a piano following a burglary (the reason for this is unknown); damage was estimated to be $2,000."

After WWII, "the Niagara Township Fireman's Association was absorbed into the Niagara Township Volunteer Fire Department on January 14, 1946."[4]

The old firehall building on Four Mile Creek Road operated from 1942 until 1985. It had two storeys with a central fire pole. The building had been renovated several times over the years, including excavation of the floor to allow newer vehicles enough headroom to drive in and out. A new firehall was built in 1984 at the corner of Warner and Tanbark roads. The old building was sold to the Rigas family, who remodelled it and named it "The Old Firehall Restaurant" and it continues to operate today.

The St Davids firefighters celebrated their seventy-fifth anniversary in June 2016, the same year a children's play area was built behind the firehall on Warner Road.

Photograph courtesy: Niagara-on-the-Lake Fire Dept.

NIAGARA TOWNSHIP FIREMEN 1942

Front Row: E. Ruston, Asst. Chief A. Sheppard, H. Evans, W. Hunter, C. Kitchen, G. Mason, L. Clark, G Jerman, R. Lambert, Asst. Chief R. Brady, W. Murray, L. Silverthorn, Chief J.H. Parnall, Asst. Chief Hugh Barker.
Back Row: B. Slingerland, H. Dick, T. Murdoch, C. Good, P. Henderson, C. Wilson, W. Fedorkow
Absent from Photo: G. Paxton, J. Dick, E. Staines, J. McCausland.

Photograph courtesy: Niagara-on-the-Lake Fire Dept.

ST DAVIDS FIRE CREW 2011

Left to right: Captain Dave Rigby, District Chief Frank Pearson, firefighter Rick Ignatczyk.
Top of truck: Firefighter Scott Pearson, Assistant District Chief Darren Trostenko, firefighter Rob (Stretch) MacLeod, firefighter Dave Ignatczyk.

(The photograph, taken in 2011, is a 1986 Superior on a Ford chassis that was donated to a fire department in the Dominican Republic.)

15

Sports

St Davids Athletic Association (1930-40s): The St Davids Wild Cats Crest is from a jersey of the St Davids Wildcats hockey team.

There were three outdoor ice rinks in St Davids: one beside the Pringle/Turnbull house, now the Rigby home; one along Four Mile Creek below the David Secord house; and one at St Davids School. Games were played against surrounding communities, including Homer and Niagara-on-the-Lake. Fundraising dances were also held at the Oddfellows Hall.

The upper loft of Duggan's barn was a hub for many sporting activities over many generations. These activities included boxing, ball hockey, and basketball. The St Davids Athletic Association sponsored a baseball team that competed against several local communities. Home games were played at the St Davids School. Mr. Jimmy Murdoch and his son Harry both coached the team in the 1950s and 1960s. When the Virgil sports field and Centennial Arena were constructed, sporting activities became more centralized.[8]

The St Davids Golf Club was built by Lynn Usher and Sam Prest. It opened on Victoria Day weekend in 1932. Shortly afterward, Sam decided not to be a partner anymore. Lynn and his wife, Jane, operated the course until the early 1960s, when Fred Hardwicke bought it. Then in 1985, the club was bought by Jack and Barbara Lowrey. Jack had been a golfer at the club since he was eleven years old and was the first Niagara resident to win a major golf tournament. He was a member of the 1953 Ontario Junior Golf Team that won the Canadian Interprovincial Willingdon Cup. He played in the US Junior Championship and the Mid-Atlantic Junior Championship. In 1956, Jack won the Ontario Amateur Championship and played in the Canadian Open in 1972. He continues to own and operate St Davids Golf Club to the present day.[69]

1934 Membership Application

Courtesy: Ian Goring

Jack Lowrey putting on the 9th green 1956

Courtesy: Ian Goring

Golf Course in the early 1930s (United Church in the background)
Courtesy: Richard Woodruff

For the fishermen in the vicinity's midst, Four Mile Creek was a good place to catch brook trout up to the 1960s. Jesse Ruley wrote the following in a 1956 paper presented to the Ontario Historical Society:

> "From the sand hills of [the] Escarpment flows a small creek of crystal clear water, the Four Mile Creek. This little stream, whose source is the bubbling springs and flowing wells of the Ravine, hides in its limpid waters the wary trout and along its banks may be seen beds of succulent spicy, water cress."

16

A POLICE VILLAGE

A police village was a form of municipal government used in the province of Ontario in the nineteenth and early twentieth centuries for communities that did not meet government criteria to be called a village. Following the Baldwin Act in 1849, a law was passed in 1850 for "police villages" to be created, and this law continued until 1965.

In 1923, St Davids was made up of Lot 89 and parts of Lots 90 to 96, including its roads. Its population was above 150, and its area covered no more than 500 acres. St Davids therefore met the criteria to become a police village. Its residents successfully presented a petition to the local council, and on July 17, 1923 the Municipal Corporation of the County of Lincoln passed and adopted, Bylaw No. 746, which named St Davids as the Police Village of St Davids. On August 20, a meeting was held at St Davids School to elect village trustees, and through their efforts street lights and a new water system were installed and sidewalks began to be maintained.[42]

In 1952, the Canadian Canners Ltd., turned their water line over to the village trustees and a larger line with fire hydrants was installed.[67] Village trustee documentation has not been kept over the years, but the following names have been remembered by elders in the village: Edwin David Lowrey, Frederick Augustus Goring, Frederick Stuart Goring, and Mrs. Duggan.

Police villages ended with provincial acts creating new municipalities. The responsibilities shifted to other boards, or the municipality to which the police village was amalgamated. In 1970, the Niagara Township, which included St Davids, was combined with the Town of Niagara to form the regional municipality of Niagara-on-the-Lake. With this change, St Davids was no longer a police village.

17

St Davids Properties

Early settlers first built rough log-timber dwellings that were later replaced by bigger homes that reflect the unique history of the time. The style of construction depended on the era they were built—for example, Georgian (George III), Victorian (Queen Victoria), and Edwardian (Edward VII).

Homes and businesses were built by families such as the Secords, Woodruffs, Clements, and Lowreys. Some of their descendants continue to reside in the village today. Many of the properties have been lovingly restored, retaining their character and style. Some homes are designated heritage properties under the Ontario Heritage Act, Part IV. Descriptions of these and other historic properties are included in this chapter.

Locust Hall, 1 Paxton Lane

Photograph courtesy: John Donald Foley

Locust Hall—so named because of the many locust trees in the area—has been owned and occupied by the Woodruff family for five generations. It was built between 1820 and 1824 in the Georgian style, with red brick. It has five bays and a gable roof. The gable ends have fan ornaments. There are two chimneys that are both connected to a variety of fireplaces. The walls are built of brick and laid in Flemish bond fashion, i.e., alternate headers and "sketcher" sides and ends, with stone quoins at the corners, and stone lintels and sills for windows. The quoins have Queenston Quarry trademark notches all around them that predate the 1840s.

In recent times, Locust Hall has been the home of Paul Woodruff, son of Francis, grandson of Richard Napoleon, and great grandson of Richard (King Dick), who was the eldest son of Ezekiel Woodruff. The current owners are Richard and Dorothy Woodruff. Richard is the fifth generation to live in Locust Hall.[29]

46 Paxton Lane, Secord-Paxton House ~1785, Bylaw No. 4831-15

Photographs courtesy:
G.F. Walker

Archaeological site near Secord-Paxton House 2017

The house predates the War of 1812—one of only two St Davids buildings that do—and is a one-and-a-half-storey original Georgian building with a five-bay-façade narrow door. It is built of fieldstone masonry, and has a harled surface rendered in limestone. The very early wooden beams in the basement are hand-hewn and still have bark on them. It also has the original window-opening locations and sizes.

The land on which it was built, Lot 90, can be traced back to Crown land deeded to Peter Secord in 1798.[25] By that time, he had already moved to the Long Point Settlement on Lake Erie[52] and, in 1799, he granted the land to David Secord Jr., who a few weeks later granted it to David Secord Sr. (Major David Secord).[25] The land was originally meant to be part of a 600-acre land grant allocated to Peter by General Powell at Fort Niagara in 1780, but it was contested, and he received only part of it. After Major David Secord took ownership of the land, he built this house and lived there until he died in 1844. The house survived the burning of St Davids in 1814. Later Riall and Elijah Secord inherited the property from David. Sometime after this, Flotyes Secord owned it and sold it to David Hanniwell in 1873. The Hanniwells owned the property until 1915, when they sold it to the Paxton family; their descendants owned the property until approximately 2008. It is now in a derelict condition and located on a significant archaeological site.

N.B. A house belonging to David Secord, and matching the measurements and description of the Paxton House, is mentioned in a war claim for the damages caused in 1814 after an American attack.[66]

137 Four Mile Creek (Secord Mill), Bylaw No. 3809-04

(Top) Old Mill Inn, courtesy: Niagara Falls Public Library;
(Right) courtesy: Kenn Moody

This Secord building is part of Lot 91, deeded by the Crown to Peter Secord in 1798.[25] It was originally built as a gristmill for the British Crown at the cost of £500 (New York currency). Parts of the building date back to the eighteenth century. It is a good example of the early history of St Davids, and therefore Niagara-on-the-Lake.

Being one of the first "Kings Mills" built in Upper Canada, this building is an early example of an English farm-style or "custom" flour mill, with two runs of stones. It was never updated into an automated merchant mill. It stands on part of a parcel of the 300 acres of land that was allocated to Peter Secord in 1780. Shortly after, Peter made a request to the Crown to build a gristmill and a sawmill there. Construction of the mills was slow because essential parts did not arrive until the fall of 1783, and the mill likely did not start operating until 1784.

In May 1798, the Crown gave Peter full ownership of Lots 90, 91 and 92, and in May 1799 he granted them to David Secord Jr., who, a few weeks later, granted them to David Secord Sr. (Major David Secord). In the summer of 1806, David Secord Sr.[25] sold two of the 100 acre lots to his brother Stephen. David retained Lot 90, the St Davids Village lot. In 1808, Stephen Secord died and left ownership of the mill in trust to his wife, Hannah Deforest, until his youngest son became twenty-one, at which time it was to be divided in equal shares amongst his six sons. After the War of 1812-14, Hannah did not make a claim to the Crown for the mill and it is possible that the mill escaped major damage because it was thought to be outside the village boundary.

In 1833, Hannah Secord sold the 200-acre farm to John Murray of Stamford, who was then Lieutenant General for His Majesty's Service. He and his heirs owned the property for the next forty years. Between 1850 and 1879, David Williams, Joseph Van Every, and Neil Black respectively farmed the land. Eliza Woodruff controlled the mill until 1889 when she signed it over to Sarah Black. The Black family operated the mill from 1899 to c. 1910. Sarah Black died in 1915, leaving the property to her daughter. The property was passed on through the Black family until John Alexander Black constructed a refreshment stand on the front and it became the Old Mill Inn. It was then bought by "Ife" Stevens, who owned it until his death in the 1950s. The restaurant continued to be open until around 1972. It hosted some illustrious clientele over the years, including Joe DiMaggio and Marilyn Monroe, who often dined there while she was filming the movie *Niagara* in the 1950s.

After it closed, the building began to deteriorate, and was on the verge of being demolished. In 1989, it was bought by Mr. and Mrs. Bannister, who renovated it into a home. They worked on preserving the post-and-beam frame, the two-storey stone foundation, and a good proportion of the mill furnishings in the stone basement.[66]

167 FOUR MILE CREEK ROAD, ~1902, THE BLACK-TELFORD HOUSE

Photograph courtesy: G.F. Walker

The information on this home has been provided by Stephen Telford, son of the current owner. The house was built as a wedding present in 1902, for George Neil Black and his new wife, Mabel Usher. The architectural plans were provided by builder Samuel G. Dolson. It was built with local natural cement produced by the Isaac Usher Cement Works. The uniqueness of this house is that it is the only known surviving Usher Cement home in the area that has retained its exterior concrete finish.

The house was expropriated by the Department of Highways from Ms. Van Wheatley in 1961 to make way for Highway 405 development. Due to unsuitable soil conditions, the highway was later rerouted, and the house was auctioned by the government and bought by Mr. Kenneth White in 1964. In 2002, the White family sold it to Mr. and Mrs. Graham Telford. The house is located approximately fifteen feet from a slope that drops down into Four Mile Creek. There are two concrete moulds half buried at the bottom of the creek thought to be used to manufacture kayaks by the White Brothers of Niagara Falls.

184 FOUR MILE CREEK ROAD, ~1902, "THE PINES"

Photograph courtesy: G.F. Walker

This home is named "The Pines" after the three large Austrian pine trees in the front garden. This name is engraved on a stone plaque embedded above the door of the porch. The house was built in 1902 in the Edwardian style by George Johnston, a relation of the Hanniwell family. Local folk law indicates that Mr. Johnston fell down the stairs in 1906, at age forty-six, and died of his injuries. In 1910, the property was sold to David Hanniwell and, in the 1920s, to Charles and Augusta (née Woodruff) Sanders. A carved stone Woodruff coat of arms has been inserted in the face of the fireplace. In 1965, Ed. and Diane Wilkinson bought the home and lived there until 2005, when the Fenwick family bought it.[35]

185 Four Mile Creek Road, ~1895, Hanniwell House

Photograph courtesy: G.F. Walker

This house is thought to have been built around 1895, and by the turn of the twentieth century was the home of Margaret Hanniwell. The main beams in the basement are hand hewn white oak from the Hanniwell farm that was previously located on the south side of Tanbark Road.[35]

190 FOUR MILE CREEK ROAD, ~1872, SLEEMAN-WHITWORTH HOUSE

Photograph courtesy: G.F. Walker

This house was built by John Sleeman and is a good example of the Victorian Vernacular style, popular between 1830 and 1900. The house was sold to the Methodist Church (later the United Church) as a parsonage by George Woodruff. In the 1970s, it was purchased and renovated by Brian Boucher, and later owned by Victoria Zettle. Afterward, Constance and Cam Whitworth bought it and have made various improvements to it, including the addition of a wing.[35]

214 FOUR MILE CREEK ROAD, WOODBOURNE HOUSE, BYLAW NO. 4807-15

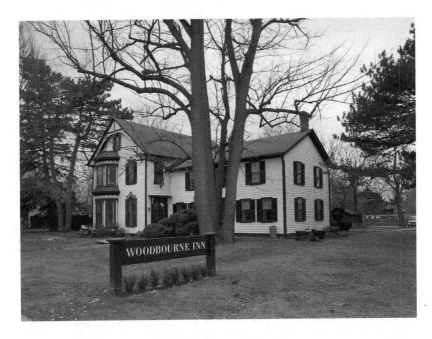

Photograph courtesy: John Donald Foley

Woodbourne—or "Woodstream"—House was named after Four Mile Creek, which used to bubble nearby. It was built by William Woodruff in 1839, and sits on part of Lot 90, originally owned by Peter Secord, at the corner of Four Mile Creek Road on the south side of Warner Road. Generations of Woodruffs have occupied Woodbourne. After William's death in 1860, his holdings were passed to his family and son Henry Counter Woodruff.

Title to the thirteen-acre parcel of land, including Woodbourne, passed to Henry's son, Hugh Woodruff. He sold it to his son Wilfred Woodruff and Julia Perry in 1928. In the 1950s, parts of the land were sold off and the remaining parcel was transferred in 1992, via Marion and Wilfred Woodruff's estates, to son Bruce and wife Gloria. They initiated an extensive restoration program in 1992.

The house consists of three sections: the original Georgian wing, the 1865 west wing, and an elaborate two-storey Victorian wing that was added in 1880, complete with high ceilings and ornate details. This most recent addition includes an entrance hall with stairway trim, plasterwork cornice, and ceiling rosettes.

The Georgian wing main rooms include an entrance hall, a north-end living room enlarged c. 1910, and a southeast corner room (library) with original trim at the staircase and baseboards and molded frames around the doorways. The east-end drawing room has an elaborate marble and marbleized mantel. In 2014, more renovations were made. The property is currently run as an inn.

Over the years, stories have featured mention of this house, including one by Carolyn Mullin, published on May 2, 1994, in the *Niagara Falls Review*: "William Lyon Mackenzie, the mid-1800s reformer who led the rebellion of 1837 against the Family Compact, escaped from Toronto and was hidden in Woodbourne where he narrowly escaped detention by climbing out of a second-storey window down a massive horse chestnut tree."[66]

215 FOUR MILE CREEK, SECORD-MURDOCH HOUSE, BYLAW NO. 4491-11

(Top) courtesy: Harry and Collette Murdoch

(Right) courtesy: Kenn Moody

The Secord-Murdoch House is one of the earliest houses constructed in Niagara-on-the-Lake. The property was deeded to Peter Secord from the Crown in 1798, and continued to be occupied by members of the Secord family until c. 1860s. Documentation indicates that the northern part of the building, the oldest, was constructed c. 1790, while the southern portion of the building was constructed c. 1830. The house has a five-bay façade and a gable roof. There are three brick chimneys. The small windows set low in the front part of the house are characteristic of the Georgian style. The entrance door is slightly off centre, which indicates that the house was constructed in two phases. The c. 1790, north portion of the home is constructed with whirlpool sandstone that was likely quarried on the property and is the earliest surviving example of a whirlpool sandstone building in Niagara.

The c. 1830 south portion of the building is built with fieldstone, probably collected from surrounding cultivated fields. It is one of the earliest examples of fieldstone construction below the Niagara Escarpment. The below-street-grade portion of the south end of the building is reported to be part of the 1830s addition. There were no field hospitals during the War of 1812-14, and it is possible that, like many homes in the area, this one would have been used for nursing injured soldiers.

The property was purchased by Alexander Murdoch, a native of Ayrshire, Scotland, in 1925, and has remained in the Murdoch family ever since. It is currently operated as an inn by Harry and Collette Murdoch.[66]

231 FOUR MILE CREEK, ~1905, ODDFELLOWS HALL

Photograph courtesy: G.F. Walker

This two-storey white framed building was built in 1905. For many years, the upper floor was the Oddfellows Hall. Here, people who participated in unusual trades congregated in a group they called "odd fellows." The idea of common people working together to improve their situation was, quite simply, odd. It met a mixed reaction from the upper classes, which saw them as business competitors. Prior to 1908 the ground floor contained a bake shop, barber shop and a bank.[35,86]

234 Four Mile Creek, Presbyterian Manse,~1903

Photograph courtesy: G.F. Walker

Henry Counter Woodruff donated land for a church manse to be built and, in 1903, Isaac Usher supplied cement and building materials from his cement works for its construction. It was built in the Edwardian Classicism style with walls of solid cement and a large, cottage-style roof. In 1951, the manse was sold for $8,000 to Maurice Irwin. In 1955, the congregation purchased a 100-by-300-foot lot from Canadian Canners Ltd., just east of the church building for a new manse. Construction started in 1957.[35,65]

238 FOUR MILE CREEK, DR. DUGGAN'S HOUSE, 1911

Photograph courtesy: G.F. Walker

The two-storey house was built in 1911 for Dr. Charles Duggan, a local doctor. The style of home is considered typical of Four-Square, or Edwardian Classicism. There is a large coach house on the property that predates the construction of the house. It was built initially to shelter the horse and carriage Dr. Duggan used for house calls. There are two stories associated with this home that have been passed down through time: The first is regarding money that Dr. Duggan gave the building foreman to pay construction workers while he was away on his honeymoon. When he returned, he discovered that the foreman had left town with the money without paying the workers.

The second story is about an attempted bank robbery in the village in 1923. A fight occurred between the robber and bank manager, and a gun was discharged through a screened door by the manager's wife, killing the robber. Dr. Duggan was called to examine the body and found a packet of his handmade cigars in one of the robber's pockets, which the robber had stolen from the doctor's home.[35]

239 FOUR MILE CREEK, ~1823, WILEY HOTEL BUILDING

Photograph courtesy: G.F. Walker

This large brick building clad with vinyl was built in 1823, and later operated as a hotel by the Wiley family. The bricks for the building came from the area where the canning factory used to stand. The building was later bought by Scottie Burnett, who converted the upper floor into a home and used the ground floor to run an implement business. Later, it became the home of Mr. and Mrs. Howard Slingerland.[35]

246 FOUR MILE CREEK, WILLIAM WOODRUFF STORE 1870-1880

Photograph courtesy: John Donald Foley

An architectural report suggests that the brick building at 246 Four Mile Creek Road may have been built in the 1870-1880 era, rather than 1820. It stands on part of Lot 90, which was deeded to Peter Secord by the British Crown in 1798.[25] Members of the Secord family owned the property until 1864, when it was sold to Henry Counter Woodruff. The building was built and owned by Henry until 1903, and is one of earliest surviving commercial structures in the village.

For a long time, it served as the local hardware store—first under the name Page Hardware, then St Davids Hardware. He sold the property to William and Carol Bannister in 1986—they began an antiques business named S & B Antiques and Collectibles. Other owners included: Margaret Doyle; Smith Bradley; William Wiley; George Joss; Annie Unis; William and Sarah Page, and son Lloyd.

Over the years, the building has also been used as a weaving craft store, a wine kit store, a café, and a real estate office.[66]

253 FOUR MILE CREEK, ~1908, IMPERIAL BANK BUILDING

Photograph courtesy: John Donald Foley

The building was built in 1908 as the Imperial Bank, and was also the home of the bank manager, who lived above it. Previously, it had been a blacksmith shop and then the Star Hotel, which burned down in the early 1900s. The bank had previously operated in the Oddfellows Hall at 231 Creek Road.[35]

290 Four Mile Creek, ~1786, Clement House

Photograph courtesy: John Donald Foley

This house was built by Colonel Joseph Clement (1750-1812) around 1786. Joseph farmed on Lots 88 and 89. The home was partly burned in 1814, and rebuilt by Mrs. Clement, by then a widow. There have been many renovations to the home and, on one occasion, an earthen blackening bottle and a child's Hessian boot were found among the fire-blackened beams; the sole of the boot had neat wooden pegs in place of nails, and was dated from the 1812 period.[50] That could mean the house survived the burning of the village in 1814. The home was maintained by the Clement family until the mid-1800s. In 1876, G. Curry bought it; then the house was sold to Augusta Vivian (née Lowrey) in 1914, to H. Dockstader in 1917, and to H. Holt in 1919. In 2007, Cynthia London bought the home from Grace Doyle.[35]

A Village In The Shadows

1354 YORK ROAD, LOWREY-FAST-PALMER HOUSE, ~1896

Photograph courtesy: G.F. Walker

A series of residences was built along York Road for Lowrey families. This house, first owned by Frank Howard Lowrey, is one of them. It has nine-foot ceilings and had a lead-lined water tank above a bathroom on the second floor that was part of a settling cistern for the house's water supply. Two sets of staircases were part of the construction—one in the front and one in the back. Another note of interest is that an underground tunnel was found to have been constructed in front of the property, running from the next-door school to the mill at Four Mile Creek Road. At one point during the thirty-five years the Fast family lived there, Karin Fast said the tunnel collapsed, and when she pushed a long stick into the hole the stick did not reach the bottom. It remains a mystery how, when, or why such a tunnel was constructed.

Mrs. Archibald, who was principal of St Davids School in 1959, lived in this house. Later, Wayne Brady and his family lived there. Wayne owned the gas station across the road. The house is currently owned by Lisa Palmer who is meticulously renovating and restoring the home.[35]

1360 York Road, Lowrey-Harber House, ~1908

Photographs courtesy: G.F. Walker

This Edwardian house was built in 1908 by Edwin David Lowrey on father David Jackson's farm. The house has two large stained-glass windows, chestnut trim, large crown moulding on ten-foot ceilings, pine flooring, cut-stone windowsills, two fireplaces, and double-wall construction with an exterior brick veneer.

The house was constructed with indoor plumbing. A large water tank was placed in the third-floor attic into which water was pumped from an outside cistern. In those days before electricity, the house was constructed with an acetylene gas lighting system. A generator was placed in the basement where calcium carbide was mixed with water to produce acetylene gas. The house had the first telephone in the village, and there is a story that Edwin Lowrey met Rose Wright, his future wife, over the telephone. She was an operator at the Niagara Falls Exchange.[35] The barn on the property was decorated in 2017 in celebration of 150 years of Lowrey farming in St Davids, which also coincided with Canada's 150th birthday.

1366 York Road, Ravine Winery

(Top) courtesy: Niagara Falls Public Library.

(Right) courtesy: G.F. Walker

This beautiful Georgian house was originally built in the village in 1802, by Major David Secord. It stands on land now owned by Norma Jane (Lowrey) Harber and husband Blair. The original house was burned down in 1814 by American soldiers, and rebuilt after the war when the village was reconstructed. Sometime later, it was sold it to William Woodruff, and it passed through the Woodruff family until 1969, when Major Woodruff sold the house to Judge Cudney of London, Ontario, on the understanding that it would be restored. Judge Cudney later sold it to Mr. Doerr, a Toronto management consultant. The new owners planned to dismantle the house and reassemble it in the Caledon Hills. They hired a Norwegian architect who meticulously sketched every room and numbered and labelled all the beams and posts including every nook and cranny to create a perfect blueprint from which anyone could reassemble it to its original state. The pieces of the house were put in storage, but the relocation did not occur.

Let's go back to 1867: David Jackson Lowrey moved his family from Ancaster, Ontario, after he purchased farmland from the Upper family in St Davids. Following his death in 1901, the farm was inherited by his son

Edwin David. Then in 1950, Edwin's second-youngest son, Howard Borden, inherited it. Howard died in 2001, and his son Howard Wesley and grandson Wesley David farmed the lower sixty-three-acre portion of the farm that he had purchased in 1979. Today, Howard Wesley is still operating the small winery with his wife, Wilma (née Van Moorsel), son, Wesley, and daughter, Catherine. The Five Rows Craft Wines of the Lowrey Vineyards produces small quantities of premium wines.

Norma Jane (Lowrey) Harber and her husband, Blair, bought the top portion of the farm in 2003, with a plan to plant a vineyard. They established the Ravine Estate Winery and Restaurant there. It was during this time that they investigated what had happened to the boxed-up Woodruff house, and found it stored in a warehouse in Port Hope. They decided to bring the house back to St Davids and had it erected on the property, where it is used as a wine-tasting room. Since then, their three sons, Andrew, Paul, and Alex, have become involved in the family business.[36]

1367 York Road, ~1815

Photograph courtesy: John Donald Foley

In 1816, this building was the home of *The Spectator*, the first newspaper in the area. It was printed and published every Friday for the proprietors of St Davids at a cost of four dollars per year. In 1817, the publishing and printing of the paper moved to Niagara.

The floor beams of this building consist of hand-hewn logs with one flat side. The framing is all mortice and tenon joined, a style that reflects the age of the building.[35] The building was later converted to a house. Howard Wesley Lowrey was born in this house and lived there during his early life.[55]

1376 YORK ROAD, LOWREY-BADHAM HOUSE, ~1908-1912

Photograph courtesy: G.F. Walker

This Edwardian-style home was built by Harry Lowrey between 1908 and 1912. The ground floor has nine-foot ceilings and features a foyer, a sitting room, two dining rooms, and a kitchen. Most of the rooms are heated with the original Edwardian-style radiators. The trim surrounding the doors is original wood, including the pocket doors between the sitting and dining rooms. The floors on each level are also made of original wood. The house has three stained-glass windows, which create coloured patterns on the walls when the sun is shining. The second floor has four bedrooms and the attic is being renovated to include even more.

Lucy, Mr. Lowrey's widow, lived in the house until her death in the 1940s. It was also home to Sid and Rita Birdsey. A small cottage on the property is thought to have been used for servants who worked for Mr. and Mrs. Lowrey.[35]

The current owner, Trish Badham, bought the property in 2010. She has lovingly renovated the buildings and runs it as a bed and breakfast called Green Oaks.

1384 York Road, Lowrey-Rignanesi House, ~1820

Photograph courtesy: G.F. Walker

The exact date of this home's construction is unknown, but it is thought to have been built in 1820. It became the home of David Jackson Lowrey and his family when he first bought the Upper Farm in 1867.[35]

1385 York Road, Woodruff-Rigby House, Bylaw No. 1481-84

Photograph courtesy: G.F. Walker

Richard Woodruff and his descendants had previously lived almost a century in this house, which sits on part of Lot 90, deeded by the Crown to Peter Secord. Part of the land was bought by Richard Woodruff after the War of 1812. Richard built this house between 1815 and 1820 to replace the original that was burned down during 1814. Following Richard's death in 1872, the house was occupied by his widow and then sold to his grandson George Duffet Woodruff. It was during his occupancy that alterations to the house were made. George died in 1900, and the property continued to be owned by the Woodruff family until 1918.

The two-storey Georgian-style house has a rectangular centre-hall plan with a rear two-storey, L-shaped extension that was expanded in 1950 to provide for a single-storey kitchen addition that fills in the "L" at the rear of the house. The front entranceway was updated in the late 1800s with a Victorian barge-board trim porch and arched eastlake Victorian double doors. Six original fireplaces still exist, and there are five period mantles with fine detail and design.[66] Ownership changes occurred in the 1940s and 1950s, when the house became three apartments. The Rigby family moved into the home in 1976. Over the decade to follow, they concentrated on making the house livable. During the house's restoration, they were aware to look out for the trademark coin that the carpenter who built the house would have placed inside the wood above a door or window to mark the dwelling's completion date. The hired worker was not aware of this, and when he found a shiny coin, he took it to a pawn shop and was offered money on the spot, which he refused. He did not realize how significant the find was until a few months later, when he gave it to the Rigby family as a Christmas present.

1388 York Road, Lowrey-Harber House, ~1913

Photograph courtesy: G.F. Walker

This house, built in 1913, has the large roof and many windows that are typical of an Edwardian-style home. The house is unusual because the first floor is built with brick and the second floor with a frame construction. It was built by Augusta Vivian (née Lowrey), and in the last years of her life, she shared it with her sister Hannah, George Woodruff's widow. Subsequent owners were Dr. Murdoch, the Erwin family, and Ruth and Ted McQuade. During past renovations, workers found a lady's purse with $100 in it that dated from the 1940s. This would have been a significant sum of money at that time.[35]

In 2007, the property was purchased by Blair and Norma Jane (Lowrey) Harber. It included the land that extended to Four Mile Creek Road and was later divided into two lots. The part that included the home was purchased by Dana and Andrew Harber, who in 2015, built a sixteen-by-twenty-foot family room and a garage.

1388 York Road Blacksmith Shop, Swallows' Nest, ~1870

Photograph courtesy: John Donald Foley

The board-and-batten building located east of 1388 York Road was originally a blacksmith shop that operated between 1870 and 1912. The foundation is thought to be much older than the building; its wooden structure was made in Stamford and brought to St Davids by horse and wagon. John Pendergast was the last blacksmith to run the shop. The building was later used for fruit packing and storage.[35] The current owners are Blair and Norma Jane (Lowrey) Harber.

1462 YORK ROAD, ST DAVIDS LIONS CLUB, ~1830

Photograph courtesy: G.F. Walker

The two-storey portion of this building was the home of Colonel Joseph Clement (1790-1867) and his second wife Anne (née Caughill, 1800-1880). They owned Lots 88 and 89, immediately north of York Road.

The home was later owned by Canadian Canners Ltd., and, in 1963, was purchased by the St Davids Lions Club. The structure to the left of the building was added in the late 1960s to serve as a Lions Club meeting room. Various changes and additions have been made over the years. The Lions Club allows other community organizations to use the facility for meetings and events.[35]

St Davids Creekside Senior Estates

(Top) Log Cabin, courtesy: Niagara Falls Public Library;
(Right) courtesy: G.F. Walker

Information on the Creekside Senior Estates has been provided by Richard and Lynn Legros. The property, once part of Lot 92 and deeded to Peter Secord in 1798,[25] accommodates a small community of seniors. In 1960, Ted and Mildred Legros bought twenty-acres from the Savage family. On the north side of the property there were eleven rental cabins; on the south side, there were mobile home lots. The cabins were destroyed in 1962/63, and the space was transformed into a campground with a pool. From 1968 to 1980, it was transformed into a retirement park community. In 2005, the community became a seniors' cooperative, and now there are 130 occupied manufactured homes and approximately 200 residents.

18

CHURCHES AND BURIAL GROUNDS

St Davids has a long history of Christian worship. *A Short History of the First One Hundred Years of St Davids Presbyterian Church*[65] describes St Davids as having only one church between 1820 and 1884. When the union of the different bodies of the Methodist churches in Canada took place in 1884, there was no opposition; the Methodist Episcopal Church at St Davids was no exception. The minister in charge of St Davids Church following the union was happy to discard old methods and embrace the regulations of the newly Methodist Church of Canada, but there were several families who wanted to retain the existing methods of worship. The question of whether the village should have another church was debated, and it became clear that there was enough support for the idea. In May 1887, a meeting was held at Mr. and Mrs. Counter Woodruff's home to agree on the organization of a Presbyterian church in the village, and the first service was held on June 26 at the schoolhouse. The two churches have since coexisted opposite each other on York Road, and today they continue to be active.

St Davids First Presbyterian Church 1888

Photograph courtesy: John Donald Foley

First Presbyterian Church Communion Set
Courtesy: Gail Woodruff

St Davids Presbyterian Church, built in 1888, is a brick, gable-roof building constructed in the Gothic Revival style, with pointed arch windows and
doors. Part of the building is built with bricks from the large smoke stack of
the James Counter Woodruff sawmill. The land for the church was part of

the Clement homestead, and was donated to the congregation by George Clement (1838-1899), second son of Joseph and Ann Caughill. It was a gift to be used only for church purposes. Author Anne Helena Woodruff was the church organist before she moved to Chicago in 1891.[65]

St Davids-Queenston United Church and Cemetery

Photographs courtesy: John Donald Foley

St Davids Church was burned down in 1814. In 1815, a frame construction of a second church began to be built on land donated by Major David Secord,[67] but because of a rift in the Methodist congregation, it was not completed until 1843. The current United Church was built on land donated by Mrs. Woodruff, Paul Woodruff's mother. The first service was held in April 1949; the church sanctuary was completed ten years later. In more recent times, more burial ground was donated by Paul Woodruff, Richard Woodruff's father. The entire cemetery is well maintained and has many early pioneer graves. The earliest discernable gravestone is for Solomon Quick, who died in 1823. Many gravestones belong to members of the Secord, Lowrey, Woodruff, Clement, Hanniwell, Slingerland and Stewart families.[35]

Major David Secord

Photograph courtesy: John Donald Foley

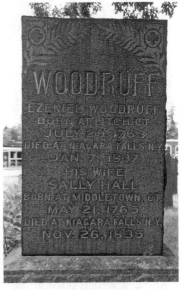

Ezekiel Woodruff

Photograph courtesy: John Donald Foley

Howard Slingerland & Melissa Warner
Photograph courtesy: John Donald Foley

CLEMENT BURIAL GROUND #1

Col. Joseph Clement and Ann Caughill
Photograph courtesy: John Donald Foley

The cemetery is located behind the church next to the St Davids swimming pool (bordering Lots 88 and 89). It is small, and contains just two graves: those of Colonel Joseph Clement (1790-1867), and his second wife, Ann (née Caughill, 1800-1880). Joseph was the first son of U.E.L. James Clement and Catherine Crysler. After both parents died, Joseph was responsible for his brothers and four children from his first marriage with Sarah Pettit. Sarah died in 1824 and two years later, Joseph married Ann Caughill, and had ten more children. Despite the huge responsibility of a large family, Joseph managed to be a successful businessman. He farmed on a large scale, employing between twenty-four and thirty workers on his 500 acres of land. At the time of his death, (only months before the formation of the new Dominion of Canada with the coming of Confederation) his estate was estimated at approximately $150.000—an enormous amount of money in those days.[34]

CLEMENT BURIAL GROUND #2

Clement Family Cemetery-Line 6
Photograph courtesy: John Donald Foley

The second cemetery can be found on the south side of Line 6 Road on Lot 103, just west of Four Mile Creek Road. The Clement burial ground is protected by cedars on three sides. The gravestones are believed to be those of

James Clement, 1764-1813; Catherine (née Crysler) Clement, 1770-1813; Jemima Clement, 1813-1813; Caroline Clement, 1811-1813; Sarah (née Pettit) Clement, 1793-1824; and Martha (née Pettit) Clement, 1769-1828.[34]

WARNER CEMETERY (METHODIST EPISCOPAL CHURCH CEMETERY) BYLAW 1271-82

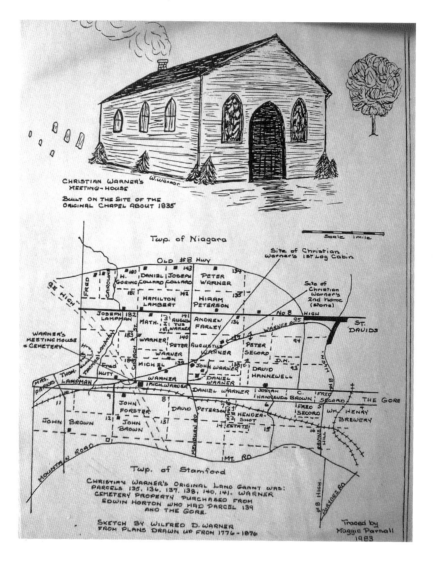

The Warner Methodist Episcopal Cemetery is on part of Lot 139, located on Warner Road, west of Concession Road 6, beside the QEW. The Bylaw designates the property as being of historical value and interest. The older part of the graveyard contains graves of several early settlers of U.E.L. descent as well as six members of Butler's Rangers. The cemetery is beautifully kept and contains a grave and headstone for Christian Warner and his wife, Charity. Warner children are also buried there, although the information on the headstones has been eroded by time. More information on the Warner family can be found in Chapter 3.[12,66]

Photographs courtesy: John Donald Foley

CRYSLER BURIAL GROUND

West of Four Mile Creek Road near Line 8 (Lot 85) is the site of a small Crysler family burial ground with six graves. This is one of the earliest non-First Nations gravesites in this area.[20]

19

Lineages of Principal Families
of St Davids and Vicinity

St Davids has a very rich heritage, and there is no better way to illustrate it than to trace the history of families that had a significant role in its development. The lineages of six St Davids families are summarized in this chapter. Ancestors who have a direct line to descendants currently living in St Davids and vicinity are presented in bold text. Generation designations are included in the form (Gn), where "n" is the generation number. Different families define generation numbers in different ways, either by counting the first generation (G1) from the original immigrant, or from the immigrant's Canadian-born children.

Birth, death, and marriage dates are included when available. If an ancestor was married more than once, this is shown as "married (1)" and "married (2)."

Francis Goring

Francis Goring arrived at Fort Niagara from England via Montreal in 1776. A talented young man, he became a businessman, farmer, land agent, secretary to Robert Hamilton, and the first teacher in the area. In the early 1780s he married and obtained a land grant and settled in the St Davids vicinity[7] (more information on Francis' life can be found in Chapter 7). Descendants of Francis continue to live in St Davids to this day.[7]

(G1) Francis Goring (1755-1842), married in c. 1781 Lucy Secord (1763-1801), a daughter of Peter Secord. Francis and Lucy had ten children:

1. Charlotte (1782-death unknown), married a Mr. Cushman
2. Elizabeth (1784-1869), married in 1799 William Parnall (1772-1832)
3. Frederick Augustus (1786-1868), married in 1805 Ann Hostetter (1786-1850)
4. **Francis Anselm (twin) (1788-1892), married in 1827 Edy Anna Mann (1809-1845)**
5. Lucy (twin) (1788-death unknown)
6. Frances Sophia (1790-death unknown), married in 1833 David Millard
7. Arthur (1792-death unknown)
8. Mary Ann (1794-death unknown), married (date unknown) Sergeant Jacob Darby (1792-1866)
9. Abraham Hamilton (1795-1875)
10. Lucretia Caroline (1799-1872), married (date unknown) Robert Lambert (1795-1873)

(G2) Francis Anselm Goring (1788-1892), fourth child of Francis Goring and twin of Lucy

(G3) John B. Goring (1823-1903), married Bersheba Cudney (1829-1907)

(G4) Frederick Augustus Goring (1855-1912), married Christina Cavers (1858-1940)

Frederick Augustus was a warden of Lincoln County in 1902.

(G5) Charlton Cavers Goring (1893-1970), married Viola Mary Stewart (1892-1971)

(G6) Frederick Stewart Goring (1923-1989), married Margaret E. Warren (1923-2011)

For many years, Frederick Stewart Goring was active in municipal politics, and became a councillor, deputy reeve, and reeve in Niagara Township.

In 1968, he became warden of Lincoln County. In 1970, the Niagara Township and the Town of Niagara merged to form the regional municipality of Niagara-on-the-Lake. From 1970 to 1973, Frederick Stewart was the first lord mayor of this new municipality.

(G7) Frederick Dennis Goring married Debbie Lowrey
They have three children:
(G8) Leigh, Ian and Andrew

Donald Muir Henderson, QC

The lineage of Donald Muir Henderson, QC, now living in Thorold, Ontario, is traced back to the Clement family. In the early 1780s, the Clements were one of the displaced Loyalist families that were granted land in St Davids and vicinity.[68]

Ludovicus (Lewis) Cobes Clement (1725-1781), married in 1748 Catherine Eliza Poutman (1726-1807).[65]

Lewis was a faithful employee of Sir William Johnson in the Indian Department during his lifetime, including during the American Revolutionary War. Lewis died in 1781 while at Fort Niagara. It is not known if he died from battle or of natural causes. He and Catherine had five children:

1. Joseph (1750-1812), married in 1784 Mary Duffet (1766-1845)
2. Jemima Elizabeth, (1755-death unknown), married c.1783 Samuel Thompson
3. John Putnam (1759-1845), married in 1779 (1) Margaret Crysler, married in 1786 (2) Mary Ball
4. **(G1) James (1764-1813), married in 1786 Catherine Crysler (1770-1813)**
5. Mary Anne (1769-1804), married c.1792 Andrew Butler

(G1) James Clement (fourth child of Lewis Cobes)[68] **and Catherine Crysler had eleven children:**

1. Mary (1788–death unknown), married Alexander Stevens
2. **(G2) Joseph (1790-1867), married in 1814 (1) Sarah Pettit (1793-1824), married in 1826 (2) Ann Caughill (1800-1880)**

3. John Putnam (1792-1872), married Rebecca Markle
4. Samuel Thompson (c.1795-death unknown), married in 1824 (1) Martha Porter, married in 1834 (2) Sarah Hart
5. Lewis James (1798-1873), married Abigail Emmett
6. Adam Crysler (c. 1800-1884), married in 1823 Catharine Markle
7. William (1802-1849)
8. George Miller (1807-1874), married in 1830 Sophia Malvina Cain
9. Robert Addison (1810-1889), married in 1837 (1) Catherine Caughill, married (2) Jane Wallace
10. Caroline (1811-1813)
11. Jemima (1813-1813)

(G2) Joseph Clement, second child of James Clement and Catherine Crysler, and first wife Sarah Pettit had four children:[68]

1. James Nelson (1815-1855), married in 1841 Eliza Ann Fields
2. Mary Anne (1818-1880), married in 1839 William Ball
3. Maria (1820-1900), married in 1841 James Durham Fields
4. Priscilla (1823-1904), married 1849 James Bigger

(G2) Joseph Clement and second wife Ann Caughill had ten children:

Col. Joseph Clement 1790-1867   *Ann Caughill 1800-1880*

Photographs courtesy: Richard Rusk

1. Joseph (1827-1917), married in 1871 (1) Frances Butler, married in 1875 (2) Catherine Butler
2. Sarah (1829-1881), married in 1848 William Gilbert Field
3. **(G3) Elizabeth (1830-1897), married in 1854 Thomas Hiscott (1826-1903)**
4. Catherine (1832-1914), married in 1857 John Crysler
5. Amanda Caroline (1834-1911), married in 1859 Johnson Butler
6. Margery (1835-1911), married in 1868 Leonard Crysler
7. George (1838-1899), married in 1864 Elizabeth Margaret Caughill
8. Augusta Ball (1840-1924), married in 1861 Francis Wickendon [Wood]
9. Rebecca Jessie (1841-1920), married in 1868 James Collard
10. Ursula Ann (1843-1929), married in 1866 William Read Butler

(G3) Elizabeth, the third child of Joseph Clement and Ann Caughill, and Thomas Hiscott had six children:
1. Joseph Edward (1854–1857)
2. Richard Mortimer (1856–1857)
3. Mary Ann Amanda (1858–1944)
4. Elizabeth Jessie (1860–1940), married in 1911 James Edward Lavell (died 1941)
5. Aramintra Sarah (1862–1910)
6. **(G4) Margery Augusta (1865-1953), married in 1890 John Muir (1857-1946)**

(G4) Margery Augusta and John Muir had three children:
1. Bertha Maud (1891-1957), married in 1915 Robinson James Richard Secord (1890-1980)
2. Jessie Gladys (1905-1993), married in 1929 Harry Connell Vrooman (1905-1982)
3. **(G5) Edna Irene (1906-1995), married in 1934 Edward Montgomery Henderson (1902-1984)**

(G5) Edna Irene and Edward Montgomery had three children:
1. **(G6) Donald Muir Henderson, QC (1936-)**

2. (G6) John Elliott Henderson (1942-)
3. (G6) Gordon Graham Henderson (1944-2010)

DON SLINGERLAND

Don Slingerland, a long-time resident of St Davids, is a descendant of Teunis Slingerland.[32]

Don and Virginia Slingerland
Courtesy: Slingerland family

Teunis Cornelise Slingerland (1617–death unknown) arrived from Holland, settling near Albany, New York in 1654, married (1) Engeltie Bradt, (2) Gertrude Bricker in 1684.

Teunis' son Arent (1664-1713), married (1) Celia (last name unknown), (2) Gertrude Van Vorst. Arent and Celia/Gertrude had seven children.

Arent's son Teunis (1694 [1684]–death unknown), married Elizabeth Vander Zee in 1719.

Teunis' son Teunis, (Anthony) (1723-1794), married Clartje Clute in 1751. Anthony came to Canada in 1783 with his wife and five children (more information on Anthony's life can be found in Chapter 3).

(G0) Anthony's son Richard [Dirk] (1759-death unknown), married Elizabeth Van Alstine. Richard served for six years with the Butler's Rangers during the American Revolution, and in the militia at Niagara during the War of 1812-14. He received 1-acre of land at Niagara, and later was granted 200 acres in Grantham Township.

(G1) Richard's son John (1797-1852), married Catharine Elizabeth (last name unknown). John farmed the north half of Lot 13, Concession 6, Grantham Township. He is buried a few kilometres from St Davids at Homer Cemetery.

(G2) John's son Richard (1830-1891), married in 1854 Georganna Oster-hout. Richard farmed Lot 13 in Grantham and then Lot 81 in Niagara. He is buried at Homer Cemetery.

(G3) Richard's son Melburn Hyram (1860-1920), married in 1879 Anna Catharine Russell (1853-1937). He farmed Lot 80 in Niagara Township.

(G4) Melburn's son Howard (1886-1975), married in 1906 Melissa Alberta Warner (1886-1977) (information on Howard's life in St Davids can be found in Chapter 9). He and Melissa had three children, the youngest being Donald Harry.

(G5) Howard's son Donald ("Don") Harry Slingerland was born in St Davids in 1929. Don's siblings: Mona (1908-2004) and Carl (1914-1983).
Don married in 1951, Virginia ("Ginny") Camille Petrunick (1931-). They have three children:
1. (G6) David Donald (1953-), married Laurie Suzanne Epp
2. (G6) Nancy Lynn (1955-), married Kent Diamond
3. (G6) Gregory Howard (1960-2016), married Jennifer Sumner

RICHARD JACKSON WOODRUFF

Richard and Dorothy Woodruff

Photograph courtesy: Ian Ransberry

The lineage of the Woodruff family is traced from Ezekiel, who came to Newark in 1795, to Richard Jackson Woodruff, a lifelong St Davids resident.

EZEKIEL WOODRUFF AND SARAH (SALLY) HALL

Ezekiel Woodruff (1763-1837), married in 1782 Sarah (Sally) Hall (1765-1835).[29] Both are buried in St Davids-Queenston United Church Cemetery. They had seven children:

1. Sarah (1783-1864), married in 1803 (1) James Maitland, (2) (date unknown) her sister Maria's widower Samuel DeVeaux (sometimes spelled Deveaux)

2. **(G1) Richard Hall (1784-1872), married Ann Clement (1788-1873)**

Richard Hall ("King Dick") Woodruff
Photograph courtesy: Richard Woodruff

3. Maria (1796-1815), married Samuel DeVeaux

Maria Woodruff
Photograph courtesy: Richard Woodruff

4. Henry Augustus (1790-1864), married Olive Edwards in 1811
5. William (1793-1860), married Margaret Clement (1794-1882)
6. John (1797-1827)
7. Samuel (1800-1824), died in an explosion

(G1) Richard Hall Woodruff (King Dick) and Ann Clement had eight children:

1. Joseph Clement (1808-1899), married Sarah Shaw
2. Sarah Margaret (1811-1834), married a Mr. Swan
3. William Henry (1814-1897), married in 1841 Mary Secord (1818-1895)
4. **(G2) Richard Napoleon (1815-1866), married in 1838 Deborah Field**
5. John (1819-1856), married Mary Collard
6. James Counter (1826-1866), married Elizabeth Thompson
7. Margaret Ann (1828-1851), married Samuel Zimmerman
8. Samuel (1829-1889), married Jane Cooper

(G2) Richard Napoleon Woodruff and Deborah Field had nine children:

1. George Duffet (1840-1900), married Hannah Lowrey
2. John (1841-death unknown)
3. Richard (1843-death unknown), married Georgina Rogers
4. Maria (1846-1906), married Geo Pelley
5. Gilbert (1849-death unknown)
6. Anne (1852-1874)
7. Sarah (1857-death unknown), married Wellington Kennedy
8. William (1859-death unknown)
9. **(G3) Francis ("Doc") (1862-1936), married in 1902 Hattie May Lowrey (1869-1951)**

Francis "Doc" Woodruff
Photograph courtesy: Richard Woodruff

(G3) Doc and Hattie May Lowrey had two children:
1. **(G4) Paul Vernon Woodruff (1903-1985), married in 1942 Helen Greig Hunter (1906-death unknown)**
2. (G4) Nora DeVeaux Woodruff (1911-2004), married in 1932 John Greenhill Walker. They had 3 children: Norris Woodruff, David Franklin and John Greenhill.

(G4) Paul Vernon and Helen Greig had one child:

(G5) Richard Jackson, (1945-), Richard married Dorothy E. Parkhill
They have two children:
1. (G6) Richard Scott, (1973-), married Amy B. Sirota. They have two children:
    1. (G7) Nathaniel Gordon (2008-)
    2. (G7) Annika Rose (2010-)
2. (G6) Sarah Jean (Dr.), (1976-) married Mark Atkinson

HOWARD WESLEY LOWREY

Howard Wesley Lowrey
Photograph courtesy: John Donald Foley

Like many of his ancestors, Howard Wesley Lowrey has lived his entire life in St Davids. He is a member of a long line of prominent businessmen. Over the last 150 years, the family has been instrumental in the development of St Davids and vicinity. They first came to St Davids in 1867, when David Jackson Lowrey bought land and started farming fruits and vegetables. Today Howard Wesley operates a vineyard and winery on part of the original land owned by his ancestor David Jackson Lowrey.[36]

David Jackson Lowrey (1824-1901), married in 1849 Elizabeth Catherine Teeter (1826-1912)
  They had ten children:
   1.   Hannah Catherine (1851-1930), married in 1884 George Duffet Woodruff (1840-1900)
   2.   Ursula Augusta (1853-1855)
   3.   Matthew Charles (1855-1931), married in 1881 (1) Helen Emily Victoria Wallace (1856-1922), married in 1927 (2) Mary McBride (1872-1933)

4. Augusta Adelaide (1858-1937), married in 1902 Matthew Herschell Vivian (1867-1913)
5. **(G1) Edwin David Lowrey (1859-1950), married in 1895 Rose Evelyn Wright (1876-1970)**
6. Marshall Wesley (1860-1924), married in 1893 Suzanna Wilhelmina McWaters (1862-1929)
7. Harry Evans (1864-1918), married in 1900 Mina Lucy Danity (1871-1946)
8. Frank Howard (1866-1942), married in 1901 (1) Maud Elizabeth Woodruff (1876-1916), married in 1917 (2) Harriet Barker Wright (1881-1966)
9. Hattie May (1869-1951), married in 1902 Francis Woodruff (1862-1936)
10. John A. McDonald (1872-1905)

(G1) Edwin David Lowrey and Rose Evelyn Wright had nine children:
1. Edwin Wright
2. Woodruff
3. Wesley
4. Clifford
5. Fred
6. Charles
7. **(G2) Howard Borden (1912-2001), married Norma Niven (1917-2007)**
8. Haldred
9. Lila

Howard Borden and Norma had five children:
1. (G3) Norma Jane
2. (G3) Lonna
3. (G3) Nancy
4. (G3) Patricia
5. **(G3) Howard Wesley (1948-), married in 1973 Wilma Van Moorsel**

(G3) Howard Wesley and Wilma have two children:

1. (G4) Wesley David, (1977-), married Tanya Tkaczyk. They have one child:
   (G5) Frances Jean, (2017-)
2. (G4) Catherine Rose, (1984-), married in 2012 Stephen Mills. They have one child:
   (G5) Borden James, (2015-)

Harry Murdoch

Harry Murdoch
Photograph courtesy: John Donald Foley

Harry Murdoch is a current resident of St Davids. His lineage is traced back to Christian Warner, one of the first Loyalist families to settle in the St Davids vicinity in the early 1780s.[45,58]

Christian Warner (1754-1833) was the only son of Michael Warner, of Swiss nationality. Christian married Charity Gertrude Eckert (1759-c.1835) in Schoharie, New York in 1775. They had twelve children:

1. Mary (1779-1811), married John Fox

2. Elizabeth (1782-death unknown)
3. Barbara (1784-1812), married Samuel Jones
4. Peter (1786-1855), married Mary Van Every
5. Catherine (1788-1814), married John Campbell
6. Michael (1790-1814), married (1) Phoebe Ostrander, married (2) (first name unknown) Calder
7. Margaret (1792-1859), married Abraham Overholt
8. **(G1) Matthew (1794-1851), married Lois Ostrander (1797-1854)**
9. Phoebe (1795-1873), married Morris Werts
10. Charity (1797-1833), married Nicholas Potts
11. Kezia (1800-1814)
12. Sarah (1805-death unknown)

(G1) Matthew Warner, the eighth child of Christian and Charity, and Lois Ostrander had thirteen children.

(G2) Peter Warner (1822-1880), son of Matthew and Lois, married in 1846 Caroline Clement (1822-1897)

Peter and Caroline had ten children.

(G3) Lois Rebecca (1855-1930), Peter and Caroline's fifth child, married in 1877 John Bouk (1852-1936)

Lois Rebecca and John Bouk had five children.

(G4) Mary Alberta (1880-1974), second child of Lois and John, married in 1901 Alexander Murdoch (1867-1955). Alexander was born in Ayrshire, Scotland, and emigrated to New York before moving to Niagara.

    Alexander Murdoch and Mary Alberta raised seven sons:
1. Alexander (1902-1932)
2. John Craig (1905-1932)
3. Robin Warner (1907-1964)
4. Thomas Eldridge (1910-2000), married in 1948 Isabel Haffner (1913-2001)
5. Albert Bruce (1911-1991)
6. Ivan Oliver (1916-1976), married Phyllis Nelson

7.   **(G5) James Rae (1918-1994), married Violet Gorham. They had two children.**

(G6) Harry Murdoch, the first child of James and Violet, married Collette Harris. They live in St Davids and own and operate the Peter Secord Inn. They have two daughters.

Acknowledgements

I would like to thank all the people who have kindly provided support for this book. Don Foley, whose unquestionable talent for enhancing old photographs and other invaluable documents, and for taking many photographs in and around St Davids. Garth Dittrick generously provided two of his paintings for the front cover (including one he painted especially for the book's purpose). Doug Reid, Ron Dale, Wes Turner, Richard Merritt, David Hemmings, and Kenn Moody all reviewed my first manuscript. Ron Dale has kindly continued giving me support throughout my second manuscript. Kenn Moody provided photographs and reading material; Gail Woodruff gave me access to her collection of Loyalist papers and photographs; Don Steele provided photographs; Don and Ginny Slingerland, Richard Woodruff, Howie Lowrey, John Fedorkow, and William Fedorkow all took time to tell me stories of their families and businesses. Howie and Linda Lowrey generously provided family ancestry information. Dennis and Ian Goring brought to light the story of Francis Goring, and provided precious Goring documents. Frank Pearson allowed me access to the St Davids Firefighters' "Journal of Minutes." Laura Grant gave me photograph copies of St Davids train station. Richard Woodruff has permitted me to use precious family photographs. Niagara Historical Society staff (Amy, Shawna, and Rebecca) were always helpful. Ann Adams at Brock University was also helpful. Denise Horne, heritage advisor for the Niagara-on-the-Lake municipal office, was always responsive to my questions. Walter and Karin Fast, Dana Lowrey, Trish Badham, Steven Telford, and Richard and Lynn Legros provided information on St Davids homes. Jon Jouppien kindly provided documented evidence of the 1813 militia uniform. I would also like to acknowledge Ray Morgan for his work with map images. Last, but not least,

I thank my husband Greg, who has been everlastingly patient and encouraging throughout the time it has taken me to write this book.

Glossary

Ague	Endemic malaria carried by mosquitoes; a sickness more debilitating than deadly.
Anishinabe/ Anishinaabe Plural: Anishinaabeg, Anisinabek	The autonym for a group of culturally related Indigenous peoples: Odawa, Ojibwa (also spelled Ojibwe or Ojibway), Potawatomi, Oji-Cree, Mississaugas, and Algonquin Peoples.
Autonym	A name given by members of an ethnolinguistic group of people, its language or dialect, or its homeland or a specific place within it.
Butler's Rangers	(1777–1784) A British provincial regiment created by Loyalist John Butler composed of Loyalists in the American Revolutionary War.
Chert	Chert, often called flint, has a distinctive blackish colour. It can be shaped into arrowheads by chipping it.

Conveyancing	In law, a conveyancing is the transfer of legal title of property from one person to another; granting of a mortgage or a lien.
Cornet	A brass instrument like a trumpet.
Democrat wagon	A light farm wagon that has two or more seats and comes in more than one size.
Encamped	To pitch tents, to make a stay in a camp.
Five Nations: Iroquois Confederacy	An alliance of five "Indian groups": Cayuga, Mohawk, Oneida, Onondaga, Seneca. It became Six Nations when the Tuscarora joined.
Fusil	A light flintlock musket.
Grist	Grain(s) for grinding in a mill.
Gristmill	A mill that grinds grist.
Huguenots	French Protestants inspired by the writings of John Calvin.

Indentured	An ancient system of on-the-job-training: Apprentices sign a contract known as "indenture" binding them to serve a master, e.g., seven years in exchange for learning a trade.
Land Grant	Land provided by the British Crown to U.E.L. families.
Newark	Named the capital of Upper Canada in 1792 (renamed Niagara in 1798).
Ossuary	A chest, box, building, or a site created for the final resting place of human skeletal remains.
Quoins	Masonry blocks at the corner of a wall, sometimes used to provide actual strength for a wall. To make a feature of a corner, creating an impression of permanence and strength.
Recollect (French: Récollets)	The Recollects were a French reform branch of the Order of Friars Minor, commonly known today as the Franciscans. They wear grey habits and pointed hoods, take vows of poverty, and devote their lives to prayer, penance, and spiritual reflection. They are best known as missionaries in various parts of the world—most notably in early Canada.

Sawmill	A place/building where timber is sawed into planks or boards.
Upper Canada	The Province of Upper Canada was established in 1791 by the British Government Constitutional Act of 1791 to accommodate the refugees of the United States after the American Revolution. It existed from 1791 to 1841 and included modern-day southern Ontario.
Vrooman's Point	Solomon Vrooman fired a twenty-four-pounder gun across the Niagara River to stop the American militia from crossing on October 13, 1812.

References

1. *Niagara Township, Centennial History by A. James Rennie, 1967*
2. *A Short History of the Township of Niagara: J. M. Crysler, 1943*
3. *Washington—A Life: Ron Chernow*
4. *St Davids Firefighters Ledger Notes: 1941-1955*
5. *Niagara Advance Historical Issue, 1977, p. 10*
6. *National Intelligencer, August 2, 1814*
7. *Goring family*
8. *St Davids sports history: Howie Lowrey*
9. *St Davids Public School: St Davids.dsbn.org/about.html*
10. *St Catharines Standard, March 21, 1959*
11. *Niagara Advance Historical Issue: 1977, p. 12*
12. *Niagara Advance Historical Issue: 1978, p. 10, Jean Huggins*
13. *Newspaper Article August 17, 1951, Vol XXXVII, No. 202 (Bank Robberies)*
14. *Laura Secord: Emma A. Currie, 1913*
15. *Newspaper article: Burning of St Davids (NOTL Museum Newspaper, edition unknown)*
16. *Butler's Rangers & Settlement of Niagara: Earnest Cruikshank, 1893*
17. *The Story of Isaac Brock, The Good Soldier: D. J. Goodspeed*
18. *A Story of St Davids: Harold Usher, 1980*
19. *"Bottling Works and Breweries"-Niagara Falls Museum*
20. *Disappearing History of Niagara: David F. Hemmings*
21. *John Butler Biography: www.iaw.com/~awoolley/lincweld.html*
22. *Secord family*
23. *Short story of U.E.L.: Ann Mackenzie*
24. *History of Niagara: Janet Carnochan*
25. *Sheubel Welton Papers: Ottawa Archives Map No. 25-1784*

26. *William Kirby biography: 2003-2017, University of Toronto Vol. 13*

27. *The Civil War of 1812: Alan Taylor*

28. *Laura Secord: The Legend and the Lady: Ruth McKenzie*

29. *Woodruff family-A Woodruff Genealogy: Norris Counsell Woodruff*

30. *Upper Canada and Simcoe: Roger Hall*

31. *NHS No. 4, United Empire Loyalists*

32. *Slingerland family*

33. *Pierre Berton's War of 1812*

34. *Clement family*

35. *St Davids Heritage Day: Ed. Wilkinson (1780-2007)*

36. *Lowrey family*

37. *Early Life in Upper Canada: Edwin C. Guillet*

38. *Neutral People, First Nations: The Canadian Encyclopedia.ca*

39. *Mitchell & Co. Directory of St. Catharines, & Gazetteer of Lincoln and Welland, 1865, p. 118 (Towns and Villages)*

40. *Land Purchase 1781, Treaty of 1781, No. 381: (aadnc-aadnc.gc.ca)*

41. *Sullivan-Clinton Campaign, 1779: Timothy Shaw, 2004*

42. *Police Village of St Davids: Bylaw No. 746, NHS Public Library*

43. *Refugees of Niagara 1779-1780: Timothy Shaw, 2004*

44. *St Davids Railway Station: Curtesy Laura Grant*

45. *Christian Warner—A Methodist: Mrs. Stanley C. Tolan*

46. *Queenston Quarry: Frank Racioppo Documents*

47. *First Peaches in Niagara: NHS.museum/medi/nhs 36.pdf*

48. *St Davids Buried Gorge, Niagara Falls Geological History: nfallsinfo.com*

49. *Niagara River/The meaning of the word Niagara: http://vediccafe. blogspot.ca/2012/08/the-sanscrit-connection-river-niagara.html*

50. *August 18, 1956 Newspaper Article: Doyle's House*

51. *Haldimand Letter, September 1779: Niagara Historical Society No. 17*

52. *Property Issues on Four Mile Creek: Robert J. Miller*

53. *Queenston Cement Works: Harold Usher*

54. *War of 1812 in Popular History: S. F. Wise*

55. *Niagara Spectator: Bartemas Ferguson, Richard Cockrell*

56. *Timeline of the War of Independence*

57. *The War of 1812—Forging a Nation: Ron Dale,* discover1812.com/about/history/

58. *Murdoch Family: Lenore Joan Harris (née Clement)*

59. *Pamphlet #20 NHS St Davids School Days: 1834: J. G. Currie*

60. *Laura Secord, Heroine of the War of 1812: Peggy Dymond Leavey*

61. *The Invasion of Canada, Battles of the War of 1812: Ronald J. Dale*

62. *The War of 1812, The War That Both Sides Won: Wesley B. Turner*

63. *Life and Correspondence of Sir Isaac Brock: Ferdinand Brock Tupper*

64. *Crysler Family: John M. Crysler*

65. *First 100 years of the First Presbyterian Church: St Davids, Ontario 1887-1987*

66. *Heritage Homes Bylaws: Town-of-Niagara-on-the-Lake*

67. *United Church History Booklet, St Davids, Ontario*

68. *Generations of Clement Families: Lenore Joan (née Harris)*

69. *St Davids Golf Course: Ian Goring*

70. *Construction of a Log Cabin: www.novelall.com/chapter/ the-united-empire-loyalists-part-5/944553/*

71. *Niagara Light Dragoons: Wikipedia.org/wiki/2ⁿᵈ/10ᵗʰ_Dragoons*

72. *Methodism in Canada: Rev. George H. Cornish L.L.D.*

73. *A Farm in the Family: John and Monica Ladell*

74. *NHS 38.pdf: Niagarahistorical.museum/medical/*

75. *Proclamation of Land Grants for Early Settlers 1600-1900www.niagarafrontier.com/work.html*

76. *Directive from the British Military Secretaries Office, Quebec January 2, 1813*

77. *General Haldiman's Letters to Colonel Guy Johnson: NHS No. 38*

78. *Fort Niagara 1759-1796: www.niagarahistorical.museum/ media/02fortniagara*

79. *Chert in Southern Ontario: Gerard V. Middleton-2013*

80. *Historical Narratives of Early Canada: uppercanadahistory.ca/military/military8.html*

81. *A Concise History of the Lincoln Militia: Calvin Arnt, August 2005*

82. *War of 1812 Lincoln Militia/Niagara Historical Museum: David F. Hemmings*

83. *Erie and Ontario Railroad: http//www.niagarafrontier.com/railroadhsitory.html*

84. *Paddy Miles Train Conductor: Niagara Historical Society*

85. *Fedorkow family*

86. *Oddfellows History http://www.iooftn.org/history.htm*

87. *Francis Goring Diary Entries: Public Archives Canada*

88. *Geology of our Romantic Niagara: A. H. Tiplin*

89. Treaty of 1763: the Canadianencyclopedia.ca/en/article/ royal-proclamation-of-1763/

Printed in Canada